MASKS OF THE ZODIAC

THE DAGGER DROPPED GLEAMING UPON
THE SABLE CARPET

MASKS OF THE ZODIAC

THE GATEWAY TO YOUR GHOST SIGN

GREGORY TIDES

IXION PRESS

Masks of the Zodiac: The Gateway to Your Ghost Sign

Published by Ixion Press
Hudson Valley, New York
www.ixionpress.com

Illustration Credits
Frontispiece: The Masque of the Red Death by Harry Clarke (1919).
Architectural Illustrations: Labyrinth patterns and digital gateway designs by Gregory Tides

Disclaimer
This work provides a symbolic framework for self-reflection and is intended for educational and entertainment purposes only. The Mask-Ghost Framework and the archetypal analyses contained herein are not a substitute for professional medical, clinical, or psychological advice. Reliance on this content is solely at the reader's own risk.

ISBN: 979-8-9956217-0-6
Printed in the United States of America

There were arabesque figures with unsuited limbs and appointments. There were delirious fancies such as the madman fashions. There were much of the beautiful, much of the wanton, much of the bizarre, something of the terrible, and not a little of that which might have excited disgust. To and fro in the seven chambers there stalked, in fact, a multitude of dreams.

— Edgar Allan Poe, *The Masque of the Red Death*

CONTENTS

PREFACE

THE MIRROR AND THE MASK

In Roger Corman's 1964 film adaptation of Edgar Allan Poe's *The Masque of the Red Death*, Prince Prospero and his aristocratic guests barricade themselves behind castle walls to escape a deadly plague ravaging the land. Defiant in the face of death, Prospero hosts a lavish masquerade where he and his guests indulge in their most decadent desires. The festivities are soon interrupted by a mysterious figure in red who moves through the castle's seven color-coded chambers toward a final confrontation with the Prince.

Prospero, a devout Satanist, believes the figure to be an emissary of Satan—or perhaps even the Dark Lord himself—appearing to honor their pact and shield the castle from the plague. Gripped by uncertainty, Prospero demands to see the face beneath the red figure's mask, to which he receives the chilling reply: "There is no face of death until the moment of your own death." When Prospero finally unmasks the red specter, he does not find the visage of a skeleton or a demon; instead, he finds his own blood-stained face staring back at him. This psychological twist captures an ancient truth: we cannot escape ourselves. It is an echo of the Greek philosopher Heraclitus, who famously observed, "A man's character is his fate."

In essence, the masks we wear should never separate us from our humanity. When used with intention, they are tools that help us navigate social structures, explore our creative potential, and bring our most profound stories to life. It is vital that we approach the mask as conscious individuals, aware of both the transformative benefits and the psychological hazards inherent in the masking process. Without this awareness, the relationship shifts: if abused or worn unconsciously, the mask becomes a prison and the wearer its prisoner.

I felt the weight of that truth when my own life began to crack open during the astrological transit known as the Neptune Square. At midlife, the planet Neptune reaches a position in the birth chart where it squares its natal placement. The key themes of this transit include disillusionment, a crisis of consciousness, blurred reality, and spiritual reassessment. This transit introduced me to my own "Red Specter," which tasked me with an in-depth exploration of the connection between masks and astrology. My gateway into this study was the ubiquitous, yet misunderstood expression: "The Ascendant is the mask you wear."

An early obsession with horror films sparked my passion for masks. The masked stalkers of the 1980s slasher genre offered me a glimpse behind the veil of "civilized society," laying a foundation for me to contemplate deeper psychological dimensions for years to come. Eventually, looking at masks on a screen wasn't enough; I had to find the source. In my young adulthood, I realized I had to "chase the mask" into the physical world. This quest brought me face-to-face with the traditional masking cultures of the Pacific Northwest, Indonesia, Korea, and Taiwan. While teaching abroad, I had the rare opportunity to study these artifacts in person and learn traditional carving techniques firsthand. This period of wandering was as much an apprenticeship in the physical craft of the mask as it was a study of its spirit. Upon returning to the United States, I integrated this knowledge with a deepened study of astrology, seeking to understand the celestial blueprints behind the faces we show the world.

The phrase "The Ascendant is the mask you wear" struck me like a bolt of lightning; my journeys had taught me that masks are not mere physical objects; they are an ancient technology. While most people encounter countless masks over the course of their lives, few give proper consideration to the hollow that lies behind them. At the heart of this work is the concept that if our Ascendant is the mask, then the Twelfth House and its related sign (the **Ghost Sign**) inform the process taking place within that hollow. How one approaches this interior space determines how one wears the mask. Within this hollow lies a doorway to another realm—dangerous and ecstatic, mystical and mad. It is a realm of gods and ghosts, phantoms and specters, and daemonic potentialities that dwell outside the bounds of time, inviting us to be and challenging us to become.

A primary inspiration for this investigation was *Astrology and Reincarnation* by Manly P. Hall. In this work, Hall analyzes the sign on the Twelfth House cusp to gain insight into previous incarnations and the karma brought forth into the present life, a technique he credits to the astrologer-priests of Tibet. He draws this connection through the study of the *Bhavacakra*, or "The Wheel of Becoming." In Sanskrit, the word *Bhava* signifies "being," "birth," or "origin," while *chakra* means "wheel" or "cycle." Traditionally painted on the walls of Buddhist monasteries, the *Bhavacakra* depicts the elements of karma and rebirth to the initiated and uninitiated alike.

By making explicit connections between its twelve *nidānas* (the links of dependent origination) and the twelve signs of the zodiac, Hall examines the law of causality between the signs: how Pisces "causes" Aries, and Aries "causes" Taurus. This concept of causality is vital to the technology of masks; it is ultimately the masker's relationship to the unconscious that "causes" the mask.

This work is made possible by the giants of the past and present: the seekers who keep the sacred flame alight. This is not a gospel, but an exercise in imagination and a doorway into possibility. My highest hope is that this work inspires more questions than it provides answers, inviting the reader into the mask and its infinite mystery.

HOW TO USE THIS BOOK

MAPPING THE MASK

Before navigating the twelve houses, identify your celestial architecture. In this symbolic system, the zodiac is read as a continuous sequence, where each sign carries a relational position to the Ascendant. This work focuses on the relationship between the sign on your **Ascendant** (The Mask) and the sign in your **Twelfth House** (The Ghost).

1. Find Your Mask: Locate your Ascendant (Rising Sign)—the sign rising on the eastern horizon at the moment of birth. This is your **Mask:** the structural facade and interface designed to navigate the physical world. *(Note: An exact birth time is required to map this position.)*

2. Locate Your Ghost: Identify the sign that falls on the cusp of your Twelfth House. This is your **Ghost:** the substructure and subconscious force operating behind the facade of the Mask.

The Architectural Tension In the following chapters, we explore the friction between these two points. While the Mask seeks to build, the

Ghost often seeks to dissolve. Understanding this relationship is the key to mastering the Labyrinth of your own design.

3. The Quick-Reference Key: Locate your Rising Sign in the first column to identify your Mask, and find its corresponding Twelfth House sign to discover your Ghost.

RISING SIGN	THE MASK	GHOST SIGN	THE GHOST
Aries	The Warrior	Pisces	The Mystic
Taurus	The Farmer	Aries	The Warrior
Gemini	The Storyteller	Taurus	The Farmer
Cancer	The Caretaker	Gemini	The Storyteller
Leo	The Monarch	Cancer	The Caretaker
Virgo	The Servant	Leo	The Monarch
Libra	The Lover	Virgo	The Servant
Scorpio	The Investigator	Libra	The Lover
Sagittarius	The Philosopher	Scorpio	The Investigator
Capricorn	The Elder	Sagittarius	The Philosopher
Aquarius	The Outlaw	Capricorn	The Elder
Pisces	The Mystic	Aquarius	The Outlaw

NAVIGATING TECHNICAL BORDERS

While most will follow the standard sequence, some celestial architectures present unique challenges. If your chart features an "Interception" (a sign veiled within a house) or if your Mask and Ghost share the same sign, your path involves a deeper process of definition and surrender. You will find the specific protocols for navigating these "Veiled Signs" and "Shared Signs" in the technical deep-dive of **Chapter 4.** For now, remember that every path is valid; as Zen Master Ikkyū Sōjun noted:

> *"Many paths lead from the foot of the mountain, but at the peak we all gaze at the single bright moon."*

PART I

THE MYSTERY WITHIN THE MASK

1

NO GOD IS NEARER THAN HE

TRAGIC ORIGINS

To explore the enigma of the mask requires a plunge into the depths of the unconscious. But man was not made to live at the bottom of the sea. The ancients were well aware of the dangers posed by extremes. In the East, the Buddha preached the Middle Way; in the West, Aristotle taught the Golden Mean. In Ovid's *Metamorphoses*, the great inventor Daedalus warned his son, Icarus:

> *I warn you, Icarus, to fly in a middle course, lest, if you go too low, the water may weight your wings; if you go too high, the fire may burn them. Fly between the two.*[1]

This wisdom was etched into the very stones of antiquity: the Temple of Apollo at Delphi cautioned, *Mēden agan*, "Nothing in excess," while Cleobulus, one of the Seven Sages, declared, *Pan metron ariston*, "Everything in measure."

---

1. Ovid, *Metamorphoses*, trans. Frank Justus Miller (Cambridge, MA: Harvard University Press, 1916), 421.

Yet, while these traditions emphasized moderation, ancient cultures also recognized a sacred wisdom in excess. This was most vividly expressed through hubris: not merely excessive pride, but a man's disregard for his fixed position in the cosmic order. Hubris inevitably preceded the tragic hero's downfall, an arc that resulted in catharsis for the audience. Derived from the Greek *kathairein* (καθαίρειν), "to purge" or "to cleanse," catharsis was the emotional release found through the witnessing of a hero's plight. By experiencing pity and terror from the safety of the theater, tragic drama expelled stagnant fears, facilitating a communal rebirth. In this sense, tragedy functions as a ritualized encounter with the mask in its most extreme form.

The word "tragedy," or *tragōidia* (τραγῳδία), reflects this raw, sacrificial origin, deriving from *tragos*, meaning "male goat," and *ōdē*, meaning "song." Scholars believe tragic drama originated in ancient scapegoat rituals, where songs accompanied the sacrificial killing of a goat to honor its life and appeal to the gods. These tragic performances took place at the Dionysia, annual religious festivals honoring the god Dionysus.

MASK OF DIONYSUS

The Greeks worshipped Dionysus as the god of wine, theater, ecstasy, and ritual madness. Linked to the grapevine, his myths are encoded with the themes of the winemaking process: dismemberment and transformation. As a chthonic deity, the roots of his vine reach into the underworld. He is a god of paradox, both benevolent and dangerous, schismatic and convergent. He could turn the *polis* upside down and right side up, blurring the boundaries between beings and compelling them to dissolve into a singular experience of primal ecstasy.

Of all the gods, Dionysus was considered the closest to humanity, and the mask—his primary symbol—expresses this intimacy. Ancient vase paintings reveal Dionysian rituals where the god's mask was hung upon a wooden column while attendants mixed wine below; it was believed that Dionysus himself inhabited the mask. While the modern mind views wine and masks as separate categories, the ancients recognized their deep ontological relationship.

Alcohol intoxication and masking share a similar subjective experience, a bond embodied in the *kylix* (κύλιξ), or eye-cup. In the symposia (ritualized drinking assemblies featuring song, dance, and philosophy), the *kylix* was the primary vessel. When a drinker lifted the wide, shallow bowl, the exaggerated eyes decorated on the exterior obscured his features, transforming the vessel into a mask. The bowl becomes the face, the handles the ears, and the base the mouth.

Scholars theorize the *kylix* served an apotropaic role, warding off evil spirits and the jealous stares of revelers. It also protected the drinker as he surrendered to intoxication. At the bottom of the bowl lay a mythic image that only became visible as the wine was consumed. In this altered state, the drinker could identify with the image, assuming a new identity and testing its limits for his own delight and the entertainment of his fellow guests. Besides being a shapeshifter, Dionysus was regarded as a god who altered mortal identity through various art forms. The epithet *Eleutherios*, "The Liberator," attested to this aspect of his nature.

The myth of Dionysus, "He Who Was Twice Born," connects wine and masks to the phenomenon of "doubling." Even today, we use the term "double vision" for intoxication. The masker's vision is likewise doubled, looking at the world through a second set of eyes. Just as the *kylix* holds a mythic image in its depths, the mask's depth houses the archetype. Psychologist Carl Jung defined archetypes as "primordial images" or "structural elements of the unconscious."[2] Our ancestors knew them as the Gods. Whether approached through wine or mask, these forces demanded reverence; Dionysus was not only a god of ecstasy, but of irrationality and chaos.

---

2. Carl G. Jung, *Man and His Symbols* (New York: Dell Publishing, 1968), 57.

THE BIRTH OF DIONYSUS

Ovid recounts that, "No god is nearer than he." Yet, proximity to the divine is often fatal. When the priestess Semele was impregnated by Zeus, a jealous Hera disguised herself as a crone and planted seeds of doubt in the girl's mind. She urged Semele to demand that her lover reveal his true, divine form. Bound by an oath on the River Styx, Zeus was forced to comply. Though he tried to temper his glory, the mere shadow of his majesty incinerated Semele. Zeus rescued the unborn Dionysus by sewing the fetus into his own thigh until the child was ready to be born.

While most accounts focus on Hera's jealousy, an esoteric interpretation suggests she foresaw that Dionysus's birth and his introduction of wine to humanity would overthrow and exile the Olympians. So dangerous was Dionysus, he proved a threat not only to the mortal order, but also to the divine order. Hera was rightfully concerned; for the cult of Dionysus took hold, paving the way for the cult of Jesus of Nazareth.

In the symbolic evolution of Western ritual consciousness, these patterns reappear in new theological forms. In Euripides' *Bacchae*, the prophet Tiresias says, "Dionysus himself, a god, is poured out in offering to the gods; so that through him humankind receives benefits."[3] This echoes the New Testament (Luke 22:20), where Jesus says, "This cup is the new covenant in My blood, which is shed for you." As Olympus fell, the *kylix* gave way to the communion chalice, and the era of humans masking as gods yielded to an era of a God masking as a man.

SEIZED BY THE GODS

Passion, instinct, and spontaneity are essential Dionysian aspects of

3. Euripides, *Bacchae*, trans. Ian Johnston. (Ohio: Faenum Publishing, 2015), 25.

the human soul. To suppress this untamed nature is to invite disaster. This is why ancient cultures ritualized the use of wine and masks. The theatrical stage provided a "container," allowing the actor to encounter the archetypal realm without being destroyed by it. Without the boundaries of rite and ritual, one is subject to "seizure" by these forces.

We see this seizure in individuals who over-identify with a single role, denying the complexity of their human nature. The ancients called this *theophoria*, "bearing a god," or *theolepsia*, "being seized by a god." This state manifests through various archetypal extremes: the inspired artist attuned to otherworldly visions is one example; the individual who loses themselves in the abyss of an altered state is another. These are merely points on a broader map of possession. Once an archetype is activated, the individual is caught in its grip, illustrating a fundamental rule: masks, like alcohol, must be utilized responsibly.

JUST AS THE ancient Greeks used the theater to contain these volatile forces, we use the birth chart to map them. In the following chapters, we will explore the popular astrological phrase, "The Ascendant is the mask you wear." By examining the relationship between the mask and the **Rising Sign**, we will reclaim the ancient understanding of the mask as a sacred tool of transformation and the silent ghost that inhabits it. This knowledge will allow you to distinguish the vital difference between wearing the mask and allowing the mask to wear you.

2

THE MASK YOU WERE BORN TO WEAR

THE ASCENDANT

Along with the placements of the Sun and the Moon, the Ascendant holds prominence in the birth chart. The sign on the Ascendant is called the "Rising Sign" because it was ascending on the eastern horizon at the moment of birth. The Rising Sign is traditionally understood to represent the way we project ourselves into the world, providing insight into our goals, our potential, and the direction we seek to take in life.

The Ascendant marks the beginning of the First House: the House of Self. Ruled by Aries, the ram, this house is associated with emergence, survival, and the descent of spirit into matter. Fundamental to navigating this terrain is the Arian principle of self-assertion. The actions we take give us definition; they become the source of our identity. In the House of Self, we speak the words "I AM" with authority, staking our claim in the universe and exercising the fullness of our being.

As the anchor of the chart, the Ascendant determines the layout of the entire house system. This connection highlights the unity of identity and destiny, suggesting that the individual and the path are one. The Ascendant is the point of contact where the spiritual meets the physical; it symbolizes the soul manifested into the time-based realm, immersing it in the living mystery. Through the development of our Rising Sign's qualities, we build self-confidence, establish authority, and partake in the great work of the evolving soul.

Because the Ascendant influences physical appearance and public demeanor, modern astrology often simplifies it as "the mask we wear." However, the ancient Greek word for mask, *prosopon* (πρόσωπον), implies something far more substantial: the undivided manifestation of an individual.[1] To the ancients, a mask exceeded its physical form; it was a composite of story, voice, costume, props, and movement. These masks were considered dormant when not in use, requiring specific rituals to awaken. A mask was understood to become fully real only in performance. In our own comparison, we may say that the Ascendant is the doorway to our "living performance." It is both our face and how we face the world. If the Ascendant is the face of becoming; the Twelfth House is what remains unseen behind it.

MASK MAGIC

To understand a mask, you must first familiarize yourself with its mythology. The mask, much like the *kylix*, holds an archetypal image within its depths. As a "primordial image" or "structural element of the unconscious," this archetype possesses its own pattern of being. Surrendering to the mask unlocks a door: once inside, the masker finds a space where physical reality and the archetypal realm converge.

The masker becomes a bridge between worlds. He stands at the threshold between past and present, life and death, giving voice to the collective unconscious. Through his performance, he engages in "reality bending"—the ability to create real-world manifestation through dramatic expression. If the masker is skilled, the audience is

1. "Prosopon," *Britannica*, 2024.

drawn into the drama until it becomes real, producing physical, emotional, and spiritual impact. A scene of death draws forth tears; a scene of triumph quickens the pulse.

If we understand consciousness as permeating all of nature, it becomes clear why ancient cultures believed masks could heal, influence weather, or alter fixed events. In many sacred masking societies, initiates could only wear the mask if they were "touched" by a dream or cured by the society itself. Only then would the deeper mysteries —the crafting rituals and ceremonial uses—be revealed.

To wear a mask is an act of surrender. When one encounters a mask in performance, the back always remains hidden. Like the grave, its **hollow** is apparent only to the one about to enter. In order to bring one face to life, another must be taken away. This relationship between "being" and "surrendering" speaks to the twilight nature of the mask. Through an astrological lens, the front of the mask embodies the qualities of Aries and the First House—animated, dynamic, and engaged. The back of the mask embodies the qualities of Pisces and the Twelfth House; here, we meet our ghosts and experience the transcendent. Both sides exist simultaneously, expressing a totality: the Alpha and the Omega.

THE TWELFTH HOUSE

Tradition assigns Pisces as the ruler of the Twelfth House—often called the "House of Self-Undoing," the "House of Drawn Shades," the "House of the Unconscious," or the "House of Trouble." This house holds insight into our conditions before birth and our hidden, repressed, or undeveloped qualities. It has long been associated with sorrow, isolation, and dissolution, linked to institutions like hospitals, monasteries, and prisons. Here we find that the urge to transcend is often met with the sorrow of letting go.

Beyond its reputation as the "House of Trouble," it is also the "House of Miracles," where significant spiritual progress is achievable. The Twelfth House, with its experiences of confusion, self-loss, and ego dissolution, can also yield profound spiritual insight. For often it is the case that man requires a personal defeat to be brought into alignment with his soul.

In the Hellenistic tradition, the Twelfth House is associated with the *daemon*. Unlike the malevolent "demon" of later traditions, the Greeks viewed the *daemon* as a tutelary spirit assigned at birth—a guardian representing one's genius and destiny. In Plato's *Symposium*, the *daemon* is a mediator between the human and divine.[2] In his book *The Soul's Code*, James Hillman describes the *daemon* as the carrier of our destiny, using his "acorn theory" to suggest that just as the acorn contains the image of the oak, each person carries an image they are called to fulfill.[3]

While tradition designates the Eleventh House as the station of the "Good Daemon," it is in the shadows of the Twelfth House where we are forced to confront the spirit's true demands. Although our *daemon* invites us to fulfill our potential, the call often goes unheeded. The word *lived* is the word *devil* in reverse. The unlived life recedes to the depths of the unconscious, where it takes an adversarial form, tempting or tormenting us. For this reason, the ancients referred to the Twelfth House as the house of the "Bad Daemon." The *daemon* is not inherently bad; it only appears so when we deny our genius and stray from our divine course.

THE GHOSTS OF THE TWELFTH HOUSE

The paths we choose often come at the expense of the paths we did not. Though these untrodden paths appear to fade in the rearview mirror, they do not cease to exist; they become internalized as unlived potentials—the shadows of the lives we did not lead. Astrology teaches that time is a circle. That which we appear to leave behind is

---

2. Plato, *Symposium*, trans. Alexander Nehamas and Paul Woodruff (Indianapolis: Hackett Publishing Company, 1989), 47.

3. James Hillman, *The Soul's Code: In Search of Character and Calling* (New York: Random House, 1996), 14.

that which we are moving toward. We are destined to reckon with the ghosts of what could have been. The Twelfth House is both tomb and womb, teaching us that the waters of our dissolution are the same waters through which we are born again.

In our attempt to grasp the ghosts of the Twelfth House, we must expand our understanding of "past lives" beyond the definition of previous incarnations. Aside from our previous incarnations, our "past lives" also include our "passed lives," previous "*un-carnations*," or lives unlived—the life or lives that passed us by. These are the abandoned possibilities, the unsolved problems, the missed connections, rejected opportunities, and forgotten potentialities that haunt us from the unknown chambers of the psyche. These are the ghosts of what could have been and who we could be.

In *Astrological Houses: The Spectrum of Individual Experience*, Dane Rudhyar interprets the Twelfth House as a window into the unconscious, revealing the ghosts of past problems and unlived experiences that continue to affect an individual.[4] He suggests that this house offers guidance on how to confront and integrate these psychological remnants. The Ghost Stallion legend of Native American tradition illustrates this beautifully:

> Once a celebrated warrior, the Traveler became a cruel chief, hardening his heart and reserving his remaining devotion only for his magnificent horses—many of which were won through ruthless deeds. He alienated his kin, abused his wives, and held the weak in contempt, preferring the cold company of his steeds to the warmth of his clan's fire. One day, discovering an old, injured white stallion among his prized herd, he maimed it in disgust. When he returned to slaughter the animal for its hide, he found it had vanished.
>
> That night, the stallion appeared in his dreams as a celestial vision, prophesying the loss of all he held dear. By morning, every horse in his herd was gone. The stallion returned to his sleep again

4. Dane Rudhyar, *Astrological Houses: The Spectrum of Individual Experience* (Garden City, NY: Doubleday, 1972), 141.

> and again, sending him on fruitless three-day journeys toward the East with the promise of their return. This pattern repeated until the years withered him; though he occasionally gained a new mount, the Ghost Stallion and his spectral band always returned to claim it. The Traveler, now an old, broken man, never saw his lodge again. He wandered forever—a prisoner of his own cruelty.[5]

Horses, like other large wild animals, are traditionally associated with the Twelfth House. As symbols, they represent the forces of the unconscious—the dreams, fantasies, and desires that fuel our behavior and drive us along the course of our lives. When modern man trades his inner life for external validation, these forces become threatening; they destabilize his desire for comfort and control. Much like the white stallion, when these drives emerge, they may appear ugly, tired, or injured from years of neglect. Like the Traveler, modern man suppresses this part of himself, attempting to kill it off. In doing so, he commits a grave violation against his own wild and divine nature.

The tired old white mare, a symbol of the *daemon* and the higher calling, then becomes the "night-mare," the untamed instrument of his undoing. As psychologist James Hillman writes, "A calling may be postponed, avoided, intermittently missed. It may also possess you completely. Whatever; eventually it will out. It makes its claim. The daemon does not go away."[6] If one does not surrender to the calling of the soul, surrender will be forced upon them.

---

5. "Ghost Stallion," in *Indigenous Peoples Literature*, 1993.
6. Hillman, *Soul's Code*, 8.

3

INTO THE CLOUD OF UNKNOWING

THE ELEMENT OF WATER

The emotional and intuitive nature of the water signs is linked to a heightened understanding of the subtle, often unseen aspects of life. While they possess a deep comprehension of the human psyche, their own motivations frequently remain obscured.[1] Like dolphins navigating by echolocation to "see" their surroundings, water signs rely on emotional impressions to map the psychic terrain underlying physical reality.

When planets reside in the water houses, they indicate drives that struggle to surface into conscious awareness. Colored by past karmic imprints and intricate emotional layers, these drives can present unconscious challenges that obstruct the realization of conscious aims.[2] To understand the masking process and the pathway of soul evolution, one must explore the tension between the conscious and

1. Stephen Arroyo, *Astrology, Psychology, and the Four Elements* (San Rafael, CA: CRCS Publications, 1975), 97.
2. Stephen Arroyo, *Astrology, Karma & Transformation: The Inner Dimensions of the Birth Chart* (San Rafael, CA: CRCS Publications, 1978), 15.

the unconscious: the delicate balance of remembering and forgetting, knowing and unknowing.

While the element of water is shared among three signs, the quality of their waters is distinct. The cardinal waters of Cancer and the Fourth House are primordial: these waters compose our physical bodies and encode a record of our ancestral origin. The fixed waters of Scorpio and the Eighth House are the waters of renewal. Similar to the floodwaters of Noah, they serve to purge the spirit of corruption and decay; only by releasing these dark waters may the soul be restored to its immaculate state. Finally, the mutable waters of Pisces and the Twelfth House are the twilight waters—the waters between worlds. They rise like mists to form the "clouds" that both conceal and reveal the divine mystery. These are the floating waters upon which Neptunian dreams are cast, mysteriously guiding the seeker on their path.

THE RIVER LETHE

In Book X of Plato's *Republic*, the "Myth of Er" presents a profound vision of the soul's journey prior to incarnation. According to this myth, souls select their next life path and purpose before being reborn. This choice, however, is followed by a crucial step: the soul's passage through the underworld and its encounter with Lethe, the River of Unmindfulness. Drinking from Lethe induces a profound amnesia, erasing the memory of the chosen purpose.

The soul enters the world in a state of ignorance. Yet, Plato suggests that each soul is accompanied by a personal *daemon*—a guardian spirit that retains the knowledge of the chosen destiny. This *daemon* holds the image of the soul's purpose like a hidden blueprint, subtly influencing actions and inclinations even while the conscious mind remains oblivious:

> All the souls had now chosen their lives... and they marched on in a scorching heat to the plain of Forgetfulness... and then towards evening they encamped by the river of Unmindfulness, whose water

> no vessel can hold; of this they were all obliged to drink a certain quantity, and those who were not saved by wisdom drank more than was necessary; and each one as he drank forgot all things.[3]

Beyond its geography, Lethe was personified as a goddess of forgetfulness. Mythical accounts describe the river's source as the cave of Hypnos, the god of sleep. In the *Metamorphoses*, Ovid portrays this scene as a deep recess where "mute silence dwells," and the murmuring waves of Lethe "invite to slumber."[4] The name Lethe originates from the Greek *Lethē* (Λήθη), meaning "oblivion," and traces back to the Proto-Indo-European root *ladh-*, "to be hidden."

THE CLOUD OF UNKNOWING

The waters of Lethe are inextricably linked to the "cloud of forgetfulness," a metaphor reflected in our language through phrases like "clouded judgment" or "head in the clouds." This motif of the obscuring cloud appears throughout classical and sacred literature. In the *Iliad*, Aphrodite shrouds Paris in a cloud to rescue him from defeat; in the Old Testament, Yahweh uses a cloud to conceal his glory from Moses.

The 14th-century mystical text, *The Cloud of Unknowing*, describes the pursuit of God as entering a darkness where clear understanding is absent. This "unknowing" is a state of paradox: to know by not knowing. It requires the surrender of the ego and preconceived beliefs to experience the divine.

This state of unknowing possesses a redemptive, miraculous quality. Aside from concealing, the divine cloud also serves to transport that which is hidden. It is a reminder that just because something is forgotten does not mean it is lost; rather, some things remain hidden until they are ready to be revealed at a particular time. We

3. Plato, *The Republic*, trans. Benjamin Jowett (Oxford: Clarendon Press, 1888), 328–329.
4. Ovid, *Metamorphoses*, vol. 2, trans. Frank Justus Miller (London: William Heinemann, 1916), 163.

experience this in the masking process: in order for the masker to *become*, he must undergo an unknowing of what *was*. It is the same process found in dreaming, where the forgetting of physical reality is the very condition required to enter the dream realm.

THE SPRING OF MNEMOSYNE

The Orphic mystery tradition introduced a complementary concept: the Spring of Mnemosyne. According to the "Gold Tablets" found in ancient graves, the deceased were instructed to avoid the waters of Lethe. Instead, they were to seek the Spring of Memory. Drinking these waters enabled the soul to recall the wisdom of past lives, breaking the cycle of reincarnation and attaining divine communion.

The spring personified Mnemosyne (Μνημοσύνη), the Titan goddess of memory and mother of the nine Muses. Revered as one of the most powerful deities, she possessed knowledge of all past, present, and future events. In preliterate societies, memory was the sacred vessel for preserving myth and history. For the initiate, Mnemosyne was the force that allowed one to maintain mental fortitude and retain sacred knowledge during the trials of the soul.

MOVING BETWEEN WORLDS

Between Lethe and Mnemosyne, a third space emerges. This is the threshold between dreaming and waking, living and dying. In *The Dream and the Underworld*, psychologist James Hillman suggests that dreaming is itself a process of forgetting, where what is "lost" to the ego is delivered into the archetypal realm as a different form of remembrance.

Forgetting, whether as a slip of the tongue or a forgotten dream, is not merely a lapse in focus: it is a pathway. A dream that resists the ego's control is a dream that belongs to the deeper psyche. By releasing elements of our conscious life and allowing them to drift away, we shift our focus from the ego to the soul.[5]

Memory and forgetfulness are the ebb and flow of the human experience. The space of our forgetfulness is our invitation to soulfulness. This **hollow** is found in the mask, the chalice, and the ego's own wounds. These are the entryways into a rich unknowingness—a realm of mystery where hidden treasures and lost potentials await reclamation.

ENCRYPTED WISDOM

Ancient philosophers believed the soul contains all knowledge, but upon taking material form, that knowledge is forgotten. Therefore, learning is not discovery, but *anamnesis* (ἀνάμνησις)—a recovery of what is already held. Imagine a ship carrying gold that sinks beneath the waves. Though the treasure is unclaimed, it remains in the depths, awaiting a return to the light.

"Encrypted wisdom" is the untapped potential we hold below the surface of consciousness. Because reality unfolds in patterns, we are destined to retrace familiar waters and be granted chances to reclaim our gold. This requires a deep dive into the "ocean of sorrows," encountering the phantoms of drowned dreams. Ephemeral flashes of brilliance—like the glint of a coin in the deep—invite us to begin the descent.

In astrological terms, where there is water, there is memory. While the Twelfth House appears to be the end of the zodiacal journey, it is also the seed for the journey to come. The past is prologue. Within the waters of the Twelfth House lie our ghostly potentials—spectral, phantasmal, and outside of time. Their cries to be "re-membered" reverberate in the darkest dimensions of the soul.

---

5. James Hillman, *The Dream and the Underworld* (New York: Harper & Row, 1979), 155.

4

WHAT'S YOUR GHOST SIGN?

THE PHANTOM TECHNIQUE

Ghost stories have captivated the imagination across the globe. Whether real or imagined, they express psychic truths that are difficult to explain otherwise. Traditionally, these stories follow a standard structure: a living being becomes aware of a ghostly presence that both frightens and fascinates, disrupting their sense of reality. If the haunted individual can resist fear and madness, they discover that the ghost keeps a secret. This secret is a puzzle of buried memory and unfinished business demanding resolution.

Recognizing the puzzle begins its resolution, freeing both the individual and the ghost from mutual entanglement. Through this act, awareness expands beyond its prior framework by integrating an unknown dimension of life—a true evolution of consciousness.

Contrary to these classic tales, the ghosts of the Twelfth House are not the spirits of others; they are the specters of our own unclaimed potential, yearning to be and urging us to become. They serve as placeholders for the unwritten chapters of our lives, making their presence known through cryptic utterances and ephemeral flashes of brilliance. To recover the wisdom hidden in these depths, we must offer these ghostly remains a "proper burial" through conscious integration. This is fitting, as the root of the word *haunting* derives from the Old Norse *heimta*: "to bring home."

THE GHOST SIGN

Turning to the birth chart, the sign upon your Twelfth House cusp is your **Ghost Sign**. We hear its faint whispers and catch glimpses of it in the dark corners of our lives, yet we can never truly "grasp" it. The Ghost Sign is the treasure chest of your encrypted wisdom: the unclaimed gift with the power to propel you toward your soul-purpose.

On a deeper level, it is the realization that what we are moving away from, we are also moving toward. In education this appears as the spiral curriculum; in mythology, as the "winding path."

For example, if you have Aries rising, Pisces sits on the cusp of the Twelfth House. Your encrypted wisdom lies in the principle of Pisces: transcendence. Behind the mask of the Warrior (Aries) is the ghost of the Mystic (Pisces). To evolve on the warrior path, one must re-member and re-incorporate the wisdom inherent in the Piscean archetype. For an Aries rising, this may look like a mindful engagement with surrender, a tempering of impulses, or establishing a contemplative practice such as prayer or meditation. Through conscious engagement with the themes and symbols of the Piscean ghost, the Arian mask gains the wisdom necessary to fulfill its potential. The qualities of the Twelfth House often appear contrary to the Ascendant, but they are, in fact, its saving grace.

THE MULTIVERSE OF THE SELF

As noted in the introduction, those with a Same-Sign Cusp or a Veiled Sign occupy a unique space in the celestial architecture. The idea of the multiverse postulates that distinct realities simultaneously coexist. Similarly, the science of astrology contains different traditions and systems that may appear to conflict, yet they all serve the same purpose—consciousness and connectivity. Zen Master Ikkyū Sōjun's insight remains our guiding compass: "Many paths lead from the foot of the mountain, but at the peak we all gaze at the single bright moon."

In cases where the Twelfth House cusp falls in the same sign as the Ascendant, the primary theme becomes Definition vs. Dissolution. This configuration makes an individual highly attuned to unconscious forces, often feeling enmeshed with them. The task is to show unwavering commitment to First House qualities while navigating the twilight waters of the Twelfth.

Because the sign's archetypes are so potent here, it can feel overwhelming. When the mask and the ghost share the same sign, the individual's life takes on a mythic, almost monolithic quality. If the individual does not prioritize **definition**, personal identity is subsumed by the archetypal theme, leaving a figure that functions as a mirror for the collective unconscious.

This is a challenging path that calls for one to become a "living ancestor who steps into the light." By distinguishing oneself from the powerful pull of unconscious undercurrents, one can learn to "read" these waters, standing in them with self-possession, authority, and—most importantly—humanity. These are highly psychically attuned individuals who must honor the weight of their gift, recognizing that an unmanaged power inevitably becomes a curse.

VEILED SIGNS

When a sign is contained within a house but touches neither cusp, it is Intercepted. In *A Journey Through the Birth Chart*, Joanne Wickenburg explains that house cusps act as doors, and the signs upon them are the keys. When a sign is intercepted, there is no door to the outer experience; one must find the answers within through a process of soul-searching.[1]

1. Joanne Wickenburg, *A Journey Through the Birth Chart* (St. Paul, MN: Llewellyn

This internal sanctuary is the **Veiled Sign**. The veil is a potent symbol of both matter and mystery. In ancient temples, it screened the most holy precinct, marking the boundary between heaven and earth. As Margaret Barker explains, the temple veil was woven with four colors representing the elements. When the high priest crossed beyond it, he had to disrobe—a symbolic surrender of his visible form to be robed in "garments of glory."[2] If you possess a Veiled Sign, you must ask: *"How must I approach a mystery?"*

Because external factors are absent, the final realization of this sign is wholly unique. Those who navigate this territory gain the ability to "walk through walls"—to bypass the internal borders that stand between them and the fullness of their soul expression.

THE MYSTIC AXIS

In Greek mythology, closeness to the gods was a dangerous affair. To engage mortals safely, the gods wore masks. In the *Odyssey*, Athena took the mask of Mentor to guide Telemachus with a human voice. In the *Bacchae*, Dionysus donned the mask of a priest to move among the citizens of Thebes and initiate them into his mysteries. Just as these masks allow the gods entry into our realm, they allow us entry into theirs; they act as the necessary bridge between the finite and the infinite.

This entry requires a stable foundation. Heraclitus observed that a man's *ethos* (ἦθος) is his fate. On the zodiacal wheel, the Twelfth House (the Unconscious) lies on the same axis as the Sixth House (Habits). This **Mystic Axis** reveals a direct correlation between the transcendent, disembodied experience and the earthly, embodied experience. To face the ghost, one must first master the habit.

Publications, 1998), 98.

2. Margaret Barker, "Beyond the Veil of the Temple: The High Priestly Origin of the Apocalypses," *Scottish Journal of Theology* 51, no. 1 (1998): 1–21.

This relationship is mirrored in monastic traditions, where prayer and meditation hold the same importance as the daily chores that sustain the physical environment. It is through earthly work that we remain humble, a word whose root (*humus*) means "close to the earth." Humility provides the grounding that ensures the safety of those who dwell near the archetypal realm. As the Zen koan instructs: "Did you eat? Then wash your bowl."

THE SIREN'S SONG

A striking example of a successful archetypal encounter is Odysseus's passage past the Sirens. Warned by the witch Circe that their song spellbinds and destroys men, Odysseus stops his crew's ears with beeswax. Eager to hear the song himself without being destroyed by it, he has his men bind him to the mast, ordering them to tie him tighter should he plead for release.

The Sirens' song is the promise of omniscience: transcendental knowledge of all that comes to pass on the fertile earth. Jungian psychologist Edward Edinger notes that following that sweet song, one might become "omniscient." However, this carries the danger of being lured into the unconscious without the ego strength to avert dissolution.[3]

In our material realm, this "song" manifests as the seeker who loses a grasp on reality through substances, or the guru who loses his humanity in the abyss of ambition. These are instances where the desire for universal totality comes at the expense of the physical body and the laws of the time-based physical realm. Odysseus survived by paying homage to Saturn. His tethering to the mast is symbolic of the union between body and soul—a state of total human embodiment.

---

3. Edward F. Edinger, *The Eternal Drama: The Inner Meaning of Greek Mythology* (Boston: Shambhala, 1994), 116.

SATURN'S CROSS

In the hermetic architecture of the soul, the mask is held aloft by two pillars: Neptune and Saturn. Neptune, expressed through his avatar, Dionysus, represents the fluid surrender and the dissolution of boundaries necessary to bring the mask to life. But it is Saturn who represents the responsibility to remain embodied. While Neptune provides the spirit, Saturn provides the vessel.

Hellenistic tradition claims that Saturn "rejoices" in the Twelfth House. This "joy" stems from a natural affinity; the Twelfth House is the Siren's realm, a place where the song of the infinite beckons the soul toward the divine abyss. To this watery chaos, Saturn brings his greatest gifts: structure, discipline, and the gravity of the "here and now." He is the anchor that prevents the masker from being swept away.

Odysseus's tethering to the mast is the symbolic ritual to Saturn that ensures his success. Whether it be a mask, a mast, or a cross, the wood represents the rigid laws of the time-based physical realm; in this wood, one finds the hidden rings of Saturn: the marks of time and endurance. The ring that binds the sorcerer to a small plot of earth is the same ring that saves him from dissolution, defines his being, and distinguishes his humanity from the realm of discarnate souls.

Similarly, it is through a commitment to the "circle of life"—the Saturnian boundary—that we can engage the forces of the unconscious while maintaining our spiritual integrity. This apparent limitation reveals itself to be a divine asset. By honoring Saturn, we ensure that our journey into the "Cloud of Unknowing" is a transformation rather than a disappearance.

PART II

TWELVE MASKS
TWELVE GHOSTS

PROLOGUE

Concerning the circumference of a circle, the beginning and end are common.
— **Heraclitus**

The hermetic philosophers of Greece, the Druid priests of Britain and Gaul, the lamas of Tibet, and the Hindu rishis of India all understood a fundamental truth: the concept of reincarnation and the science of astrology are intertwined, forming a singular lens through which the soul's journey has been viewed for ages.

The Ouroboros—the serpent eating its own tail—symbolizes this eternal cycle of life, death, and rebirth. This ancient icon likely entered Western tradition via Egyptian iconography and Greek magic, eventually becoming a pillar of Gnosticism, Hermeticism, and alchemy. The word itself derives from the Ancient Greek *οὐροβόρος*: *oura* (tail) plus *-boros* (eating).

In the *Timaeus*, Plato describes the universe as a cosmic Ouroboros:

It needed not eyes, for naught visible was left outside; nor hearing, for there was nothing to hear; and there was no surrounding air which made breathing needful... For by design was it created to supply its own sustenance by its own wasting, and to have all its action and passion in itself and by itself.[1]

In this light, the Ouroboros expresses the ultimate Divine Design. It is a self-contained creation arising from itself—a concept foundational to almost every creation myth ever told.

THE ZODIACAL CYCLE

Like the Ouroboros, the zodiacal wheel ends in Pisces only to begin again in Aries, reminding us that the beginning is the end, and the end is the beginning. As astrologer Steven Forrest notes, it is seasonal changes—not just the stars—that lie at the heart of sign symbolism.[2]

- **Aries:** The vernal equinox signifies the start of spring; life bursts through the frost; animals awaken and emerge from their lairs. This is the time of the Warrior, where the struggle for survival is a necessary fight to secure new existence.
- **Taurus:** As we move into the next phase, the initial struggle settles. Life has secured its place and can now grow into its "beingness." Flowers blossom and the air fills with song. This is the time of the Farmer, where the Arian principle of self-assertion evolves into the Taurean principle of sensuality.

We can view the signs as links in a chain, encompassing the totality of the life cycle and the underlying law of causality.

1. Plato, *The Timaeus of Plato*, ed. R. D. Archer-Hind (London: Macmillan, 1888), 101.
2. Steven Forrest, *The Inner Sky* (San Diego: ACS Publications, 1984), 30.

THE MASK AND THE GHOST

In the following pages, we will explore the relationship between the zodiacal archetypes of the Ascendant (the Mask) and the Twelfth House cusp (the Ghost). On a deeper level, these archetypes inform and relate to one another in a constant dialogue of definition and dissolution.

Each upcoming section includes:

- **The Labyrinth:** A visual and symbolic gateway. Unlike a maze, which is designed to confuse and trap, a labyrinth has only one path. You cannot get lost; you can only become impatient. As you move through these protocols, consider the Labyrinth your internal map. The path to the center is rarely a straight line—it requires the courage to move toward the darkness of the interior to find the light of the self.
- **A Poetic Imagining:** Exploring how the Mask and Ghost interact in both conflict and harmony.
- **The Mythological Lens:** Tracing the relationship through the echoes of ancient stories.
- **The Heart of the Analysis:** A distilled, one-line summary of the core lesson.

The principles I have selected for each sign are those that resonated most through my research and my experience reading charts. May this humble offering inspire those seekers interested in engaging the deeper mysteries of their own "star mask."

THE MASK | GHOST FRAMEWORK

Rising Sign	The Mask	Principle	Haunted by	Encrypted Wisdom
Aries	The Warrior	Self-Assertion	Loss of Self	Transcendence
Taurus	The Farmer	Sensuality	War	Self-Assertion
Gemini	The Storyteller	Instinctive Mind	Captivity	Sensuality
Cancer	The Caretaker	Feelings and Emotions	Doubt	Instinctive Mind
Leo	The Monarch	Self-Expression	Obscurity	Feelings and Emotions
Virgo	The Servant	Discernment	Perfection	Self-Expression
Libra	The Lover	Partnership	Indecision	Discernment
Scorpio	The Investigator	Transformation	Betrayal	Partnership
Sagittarius	The Philosopher	Direction	Stagnation	Transformation
Capricorn	The Elder	Realization	Aimlessness	Direction
Aquarius	The Outlaw	Distribution	Conformity	Realization
Pisces	The Mystic	Transcendence	Assimilation	Distribution

THE MYTHOLOGICAL LENS: AN INVITATION TO THE SOURCE

Within the architecture of each mask, I have provided a "Mythological Lens"—a brief illumination of the ancient stories that have shaped our understanding of these archetypes for millennia. However, the architect's sketch is not the finished cathedral.

It is vital to understand that the myths presented here are offered in their most elemental form. They are intended as points of departure, not destinations. Mythology, much like the zodiac itself, is a living, breathing body of wisdom that reveals different layers of truth depending on the observer's own stage of evolution.

Regarding your own study: I encourage you, the seeker and the student, to use these brief sketches as a catalyst for your own deep-structure research. To truly understand the "Ghost" of your Twelfth House or the "Mask" of your Ascendant, you must go beyond these pages. Seek out the original hymns, the unabridged epics, and the varied cultural interpretations of these deities.

Consider this book a compass, but remember: the compass only points the way.

1

ARIES RISING: MASK OF THE WARRIOR

Associated Archetypes: The Pioneer, The Survivor
Planetary Ruler: Mars | **Element:** Fire | **Mode:** Cardinal
Aries Rising is the pathway to: SELF-ASSERTION
Ghost Sign: PISCES
Behind the Mask of THE WARRIOR is the Ghost of THE MYSTIC
Aries Rising is haunted by: LOSS OF SELF
Fear Response: Impulse divorced from intellect
The Encrypted Wisdom: TRANSCENDENCE
Integration: The tiger of impulse is no longer the master; it becomes a supportive ally on the evolutionary path.
Key Concept: The Beautiful Death

GHOSTLY ENCOUNTER

The Warrior stands on the front line, war paint still wet on his face, knuckles white as he clenches his blade. The enemy army approaches, and the earth trembles beneath him. As the villagers flee in terror, the Warrior stands firm, he knows it is only by looking into the eyes of death that he finds the promise of life. His heart pounds like a drum, his blood surges like fire. He is alive, attuned, and unafraid to plunge himself like a spear into the breast of the unknown. Where others falter, the Warrior thrives, and it is through his courage that the future is secured.

The ghost of the Mystic dances in the dust cloud raised by the approaching hordes. Without armor, without weapon, she drifts toward the front lines. The Warrior stands confused. How can one be so careless and so ambivalent in the face of certain defeat? A shroud of darkness falls upon his heart. He lashes out, striking at the Mystic, but his blows never land. Lost in the violence, he who was once a proud soldier becomes a madman swinging a sword at his own shadow—defeated before the battle has even begun.

The Mystic teaches the Warrior that genuine victory is victory over oneself. It is not enough to jump headfirst into the obstacles of life; one must also turn inward to seek the counsel of the heart. The Warrior must unite ferocity with compassion and balance instinct with intellect. By conquering his inner struggles, Aries Rising gains discipline. With discipline, his instincts no longer rule him; they serve him.

NOTES FROM THE UNDERWORLD: ACHILLES

> *Sing, Goddess, of the rage of Peleus' son Achilles—the accursed rage that brought great suffering to the Achaeans.*[1]

So begins Homer's *Iliad*. Achilles, the quintessential warrior, was defined by epithets like "the Proud Runner," "the Blazing," and "the Most Violent Man in the World." Born to the mortal king Peleus and the Nereid Thetis, his path was marked by the divine. To grant him immortality, Thetis dipped the infant Achilles into the River Styx, rendering his body invulnerable, save for the heel by which she held him.

Achilles was instrumental in the Greek victory at Troy, his valor

1. Homer, *The Iliad*, trans. Robert Fagles (New York: Viking, 1990), 1.1–2.

impressing even the gods. The turning point of the epic was his slaying of Hector, the Trojan commander. Yet, Achilles met his demise at the gates of Troy when an arrow, fired by Paris and guided by Apollo, struck his vulnerable heel. Though the warrior passed into the gates of Hades, it was an ambush that took his life. He forever remained undefeated in open combat.

SIGNS AND SYMBOLS

Cardinal Fire defines the start of the zodiacal cycle. To the ancient Zoroastrians, fire was the supreme symbol of purity and the illumined mind. In Genesis, Yahweh's first command, "Let there be light," propelled divine fire into existence. In the Eastern Orthodox tradition, the "Holy Light" (*Hagion Fos*) is said to erupt from Jesus' tomb—a "fire of resurrection" symbolizing victory over darkness.

When the Sun enters Aries, it marks the vernal equinox—a time of emergent urgency where life takes extreme measures to secure its existence. Mars, the planetary ruler, oversees the development of the will. As the ruler of the First House, the House of Self, Aries represents the "door to life." To be is to dare, and no one knows this better than the Warrior.

GHOSTLY DYNAMIC

For Aries Rising, the "Achilles heel" is the gateway to their Piscean ghost. Achilles' vulnerability lay in the soft flesh where his mother's hand held him. In this **hollow**, we find the ghost of The Mystic. Etymologically, the name Achilles (Ἀχιλλεύς) stems from *áchos* (ἄχος, "sorrow") and *laós* (λαός, "nation").[2] When Achilles aligns action with intellect, his name is a testament to the sorrow and devastation he causes his enemies. When divorced from the intellect, he brings sorrow upon his own people.

2. Leonard Palmer, *The Interpretation of Mycenaean Greek Texts* (Oxford: Clarendon Press, 1963), 79.

For those on the Warrior path, the war often follows them home. This is visible in the phenomenon of post-traumatic stress disorder (PTSD), where the soldier finds threats where none exist, unable to rest or find peace. This heightened alertness creates manufactured conflicts with those the Aries Rising holds closest. It is a vital lesson for this mask to remember the old axiom: Choose your battles wisely.

INTEGRATION

The ghost of the Mystic holds the wisdom of Transcendence. While Aries rules the head, Pisces rules the feet. Reflexology teaches that all nerves travel to the feet, just as the entire zodiac converges in the Piscean waters. It is upon the sole (soul) that the foot rests. In the word "heel," we hear the homophone "heal"—to restore health. We also use "heel" as a command for obedience and stillness. While these attributes—obedience, healing, and humility—belong to the Mystic, they are the very tools the Warrior needs to train the mind.

In the case of Achilles, entry into the lowest, most vulnerable part of his being allowed him to transcend the battlefield. The Ancient Greeks called this *kalós thánatos*—**The Beautiful Death.** A warrior who met his end with honor was elevated to glory; the deed that ended his life was the same deed that actualized his excellence.[3] Aries Rising knows how to meet conflict, but only through the ghost of the Mystic does he learn to meet the "defeat" necessary to achieve the ultimate glory: the total alignment of the will and the soul.

SUMMARY: A true warrior knows not only how to wield a blade, but also how to meet its edge.

---

3. Jean-Pierre Vernant, "Some Psychological Aspects of the Heroic Figure in Homer," in *Oxford Readings in Homer's Iliad*, ed. D.L. Cairns (Oxford: Oxford University Press, 2001), 50–51.

2

TAURUS RISING: MASK OF THE FARMER

Associated Archetypes: The Earth Spirit, The Musician
Planetary Ruler: Venus | **Element:** Earth | **Mode:** Fixed
Taurus Rising is the pathway to: SENSUALITY
Ghost Sign: ARIES
Behind the Mask of THE FARMER is the Ghost of THE WARRIOR
Taurus Rising is haunted by: WAR
Fear Response: The threat of loss causes The Farmer to hold on tighter.
The Encrypted Wisdom: SELF-ASSERTION
Integration: Security is an outward expression of an inward state, maintained through courageous acts of self-assertion.
Key Concept: The Warrior Impulse

GHOSTLY ENCOUNTER

The world is a dog chasing its own tail. Somewhere in the distance—beyond the cloud of dust, the noise, and the commotion—lies the Farmer. She stands rooted in the earth, tending to her plants and animals, attuned to the silent cycles of nature. The Farmer knows that the wisdom of the body is the only true currency; if one quiets the mind, they might finally hear it. With deep pleasure, she cultivates the land, accumulating the bounty necessary to sustain a lasting peace, both inside and out.

Yet, on the outer edges of the farm lurks the ghost of the Warrior. Blood stains his face; his sword is drawn close to his breast. Wide-eyed and sleep-deprived, he circles the perimeter. His terrifying appearance reminds the Farmer that she has much to lose. The more she contemplates loss, the tighter she holds on. Slowly, the farm becomes a prison, and the Farmer its prisoner. A dull, gray, "maximum security" reality replaces the magic that once bloomed in the open air.

But the ghost of the Warrior comes neither to kill nor to plunder; he comes to remind the Farmer of the blood that flows through her own veins. His message is this: *Life is fire.* Sometimes it warms us, other times it consumes us, but it always calls us to action. When Taurus Rising follows **the warrior impulse,** it leads to her inner gold —a state of stability so unshakeable that it remains intact regardless of circumstance. The Warrior reminds the Farmer: "Live while you're still alive."

NOTES FROM THE UNDERWORLD: THE MINOTAUR

To secure his rule over Crete, King Minos sought a divine favor from Poseidon, who sent him a magnificent white bull to be sacrificed in his honor. Captivated by the beast's beauty, Minos broke his oath and sacrificed a lesser animal instead. Enraged, Poseidon cursed Minos's wife, Pasiphae, with an unnatural desire for the bull. From this union was born the Minotaur—a monstrous abomination and a living symbol of a broken promise.

Minos imprisoned the Minotaur within a vast Labyrinth, demanding a tribute of fourteen youths from Athens every nine years to feed the beast's hunger. This cycle of blood continued until the hero Theseus, aided by Minos's daughter Ariadne, entered the labyrinth. Ariadne provided Theseus with a silken thread to navigate the darkness. Theseus slew the Minotaur, and the two fled Crete, leaving the kingdom to be devastated by natural disasters.

SIGNS AND SYMBOLS

Taurus, the second sign of the zodiac, is anciently associated with the Moon, the Goddess, and her consort, the Bull. These themes trace back to the Paleolithic caves, where a primitive astrology first took root. During this era, "Venus" figurines—voluptuous stone carvings like the *Venus of Laussel*—depicted the Earth Mother in her guise of total fertility. In one hand, she holds a bison horn marked with thirteen notches, representing the lunar cycles of the year. The Bull's horns, shaped like the crescent moon, became the primary emblem of divine fertility and the central mystery of the bull-cults.[1]

As the season of Taurus begins, the Arian struggle for survival ends. What has survived is now ready to flourish. Nature reveals her majesty through the senses, ruled by the planet Venus, who oversees the harmony of substance. Taurus rules the Second House—the House of Money. While it involves physical currency, the Second House more deeply represents the internal resources and beliefs that ground our reality. Like the ancient caves of the Goddess, it serves as the storehouse for the values that imbue our lives with quality and meaning.

GHOSTLY DYNAMIC

In the myth of the Minotaur, Theseus represents the ghost of the Warrior, while the Minotaur represents a distortion of the Farmer's mask. In older Cretan myths, the Minotaur was a divine bull-man named Asterion (Ἀστερίων), meaning "Starry One." In his demonized form, he became a creature bound to a king's greed.

On a personal level, this distortion turns the Taurus Rising's life

1. A. Bancroft, *Origins of the Sacred: The Way of the Sacred in Western Tradition* (London: Arkana, 1987), 43.

into a deadening cycle of repetition. The hunger for security suppresses their wild, divine nature. It is only an encounter with the Arian shadow—the warrior who holds the golden thread—that can lead the soul from the static realm of death into the vital realm of life. The Warrior asks: "What is the sacred bull you must sacrifice to allow the growth that life demands?"

INTEGRATION

While the Minotaur represents the distortion of the mask, his half-sister Ariadne embodies the Farmer archetype at a higher vibration. Her love for Theseus (**the warrior impulse**) leads to the necessary sacrifice of the bull, ensuring her exit from a declining kingdom and her eventual union with Dionysus.

Some scholars suggest the Labyrinth was not a physical maze, but a sacred dance—a "winding way" that mirrored the spiral pattern of reality and the motion of the stars. To those who fear **the warrior impulse**, the Labyrinth is a prison. But to those who honor it, the Labyrinth is a spiral dance connecting heaven and earth, life and death.

The twisting Paleolithic caves served as ancient initiation sites. By entering these depths, the initiate experienced a "spring season of the soul," facing dangerous passages where death was a constant probability. The remnants of these underworld journeys, preserved in myths like Theseus and the Minotaur, teach us that to reach a state of unity with our natural essence, we must be ready to face danger. Nature's winding ways are as perilous as they are beautiful. To secure their own wild beauty, Taurus Rising must honor **the warrior impulse.**

SUMMARY: The beauty of a rose lies in the blood drawn by its thorns.

3

GEMINI RISING: MASK OF THE STORYTELLER

Associated Archetypes: The Witness, The Teacher
Planetary Ruler: Mercury | **Element:** Air | **Mode:** Mutable
Gemini Rising is the pathway to: INSTINCTIVE MIND
Ghost Sign: TAURUS
Behind the Mask of THE STORYTELLER is the Ghost of THE FARMER
Gemini Rising is haunted by: CAPTIVITY
Fear Response: Distraction as a way to dodge perceived capture.
The Encrypted Wisdom: SENSUALITY
Integration: Sensuality is a doorway to depth; it allows for the sustained development of gifts and talents, drawing the seeker into a meaningful embodiment.
Key Concept: Earth Medicine

GHOSTLY ENCOUNTER

Everyone gathers around the Storyteller. Beneath the stars, his epic tales of gods and monsters, heroes and villains, stir the hearts of all who listen. Even the creatures of the forest draw near to partake in the wonder. The Storyteller unleashes curiosity and activates the imagination; he is the ultimate expert on the magic of words, knowing that to spell the right word is to cast the right spell.

But a figure in the distance catches the Storyteller's eye. Amidst emerald fields lies the ghost of the Farmer. Her hands are stained with dirt; beads of sweat cover her flesh like a garment of pearls. She rises from the black earth as if it were a lover's bed. She possesses a quiet contentment—a fulfillment found in silence. This presence disrupts the Storyteller. Confusion sets in; he begins to flutter from one topic to the next, losing himself in a labyrinth of ideas that lead everywhere but go nowhere. Unfazed, the Farmer stands as still as a pillar of stone and smiles. *What does she know?*

The ghost of the Farmer reminds the Storyteller that sensuality is not a trap; it is an entry point. As powerful as words are, the space between them is equally vital. The Farmer brings the Storyteller into that space, teaching him how to commune, how to nurture, and how to commit. Like a seed, his devotion soon grows into a vine, allowing him to partake in the fruitful abundance hidden within the soul. By drinking the dark wine of the Farmer's chalice, the Storyteller experiences the *eros* and intimacy of embodiment.

NOTES FROM THE UNDERWORLD: ECHO

Zeus was notorious for bedding nymphs, and his wife, Hera, made it her mission to catch him in the act. Whenever Hera drew close, Zeus commanded a nymph named Echo to distract the goddess with endless chatter. When Hera realized she was being deceived, she cast a curse:

> "I shall give you less power over that tongue by which I have been deluded."[1]

Cursed to never speak for herself, Echo could only repeat the last

1. Ovid, *Metamorphoses*, trans. A.S. Kline (Poetry in Translation, 2000), 92.

words spoken to her. She later fell in love with the hunter Narcissus, but her voicelessness doomed the pursuit. As her body faded away in shame, the only remnant of her being was her voice—an echo of others.

SIGNS AND SYMBOLS

Just as the wind animates the sail of a ship, the instinctive mind brings Gemini Rising to life. To understand this mind is to catch the tail of a thought and follow its trail into the unknown. When the Sun moves into Gemini, late spring turns to early summer. This is the time of the firefly—creatures that shine when they communicate. Their glow, flickering like a sparkling Morse code, illumines a mystery for those daring enough to decipher it.

Planetary ruler Mercury, the messenger of the gods, oversees the processing of information and the formation of perception. Gemini rules the Third House—the House of Communication—where we develop our world-view through immediate interaction. The glyph for Gemini represents two columns forming a temple entrance: a doorway of perception. In the Yin-Yang symbol, the serpentine line curving through the center represents the Storyteller—always moving, unexpected, and ever-changing.

GHOSTLY DYNAMIC

In the architectural tension between the Storyteller mask and the Farmer ghost, we find the mythic silhouette of Echo. She is a figure of deception by circumstance—a divine interpreter forced to choose between gods. Her dilemma is a paradox: she is a voice without a body, in love with a man who can love only himself. Paradox is the realm of the god Mercury. As a substance, mercury is both metal and liquid—never revealed, yet reflecting everything on its surface.

For Gemini Rising, their energy appears as a mirrored serpent tracing the path between opposites. As long as it moves, it shines. To this serpent's tail, Gemini Rising holds on for dear life, following the instinctive mind wherever it leads. Yet, this unpredictability can run contrary to the stability required for depth. Without the wisdom of Taurean sensuality, the Storyteller captivates but struggles to connect. The ghost of the Farmer offers the weight needed to turn a "fascinating" story into a "meaningful" one.

INTEGRATION

After Narcissus rejected Echo, he fell in love with his own reflection in a spring and remained there until he transformed into a flower. Here, the Farmer archetype exists covertly. Narcissus embodies the shadow of Taurus: beautifully inert, immobilized, and transformed from a "being" into an "object." This beauty serves as a threshold; it was while reaching for these very flowers that the goddess Persephone broke the surface of the mundane and was pulled into the transformative depths of the underworld.

For both Echo and Narcissus, there is a struggle with the ephemeral nature of reality. Echo longs for the flower—the beauty and **the earth medicine** manifested in physical form. Scholars believe the name *Narcissus* comes from the Greek *narkao* ("to numb"), the root of *narcotic.*[2] Perhaps Echo's longing is to be made "numb" to the distractions that prevent her from attaining embodiment?

The potter, another Taurean archetype, reminds us that Earth provides the forms that contain our experience. For Gemini Rising, containment is **the earth medicine** through which gifts develop, connections thrive, and soul alignment blossoms.

SUMMARY: The flower that lasts a moment honors a moment that lasts a lifetime.

---

2. "narcissus," *Online Etymology Dictionary*, 2001.

4

CANCER RISING: MASK OF THE CARETAKER

Associated Archetypes: The Healer, The Invisible Man/Woman
Planetary Ruler: The Moon | **Element:** Water | **Mode:** Cardinal
Cancer Rising is the pathway to: FEELINGS AND EMOTIONS
Ghost Sign: GEMINI
Behind the Mask of THE CARETAKER is the Ghost of THE STORYTELLER
Cancer Rising is haunted by: DOUBT
Fear Response: Locked inside a suit of armor; she is in the world but not open to it.
The Encrypted Wisdom: INSTINCTIVE MIND
Integration: Cancer Rising can open their heart and trust in life; in return, life rewards her.
Key Concept: Dragon Consciousness

GHOSTLY ENCOUNTER

A wounded child falls into the arms of the Caretaker. Within her loving embrace, the child finds respite from a cold and cruel world. Here, compassion is a living principle that nourishes hunger, quenches thirst, and restores faith. The Caretaker knows the pain in the child's soul is real because she feels it as her own. Her extraordinary imagination and profound emotional depth are the tools she uses to channel nature's healing forces.

Yet, the Caretaker must beware, for in the shadow of her compassion lies the ghost of the Storyteller. With a forked tongue pressed close to her ear, he whispers tales of a doomed world. If the Caretaker allows herself to be bewitched, her loving embrace becomes a vice-grip of death. She becomes unable to let go of those she cares for, failing to differentiate her own identity from their wounds. Her dark emotions act like a whirlpool, dragging her soul into cold, silent depths. Where once stood a great healer, there now lies a drowning woman, pulling everyone down in a desperate attempt to save herself from the abyss of her own suspicions.

The Storyteller teaches Cancer Rising that we are the authors of our own narratives. Through her sensitivity, she will experience a multitude of realities. It is imperative that she honors her intuition which, like the Moon, lights the way in the dark. If the Caretaker can move through the world without surrendering her authority, she remains a vessel of emotional truth and a guide through the labyrinth.

NOTES FROM THE UNDERWORLD: JOCASTA

King Laius of Thebes attempted to avoid fatherhood after the Delphic Oracle warned that his son would kill him and marry his wife, Jocasta. However, after a drunken encounter, Jocasta conceived. To thwart the prophecy, they abandoned the infant Oedipus on a mountain. Rescued by a compassionate shepherd, Oedipus grew up in Corinth. Years later, seeking his true parentage, the Oracle gave him the same terrifying prophecy. Fleeing Corinth to protect those he thought were his parents, he unknowingly killed Laius at a crossroads and later married the widowed Jocasta after solving the Sphinx's riddle. When the horrific truth was finally revealed, it led to Jocasta's suicide and Oedipus's self-blinding and exile.

SIGNS AND SYMBOLS

As the bearer of the Mother archetype, Cancer is the ever-flowing bosom that nourishes and protects her children. In her shadow aspect, she is the Dragon—mistress of the primordial waters. The *Book of Enoch* describes the *Leviathan* as a female monster dwelling in the "abysses of the ocean," linking her to the Mesopotamian goddess *Tiamat*.[1] As the "Dragon at the beginning of time," she embodies the wisdom of creativity and destruction inherent in primeval chaos.

The Summer Solstice marks the season of Cancer—a time of peak light that initiates an inward turn. Her ruler, the Moon, governs the ebb and flow between the visible and the hidden, pushing and pulling the emotional tides within us. Cancer rules the Fourth House —the Midnight House—the deepest point of the zodiac. This house holds the roots of our unconscious programming. From these dark waters, the Cancer Rising can lift up treasures of the imagination, but they must also face the sea monsters lurking there.

GHOSTLY DYNAMIC

In the architectural tension between the Caretaker mask and the Storyteller ghost, we find the tragic silhouette of Jocasta. The myth of Oedipus is so potent it became the foundation for the "Oedipus Complex" in modern psychology, revealing the primal impulses—the vibes and gut feelings—that drive our unconscious. For Jocasta, these impulses were the "silent knowings" she chose to ignore.

When the ghost of the Storyteller is unintegrated, Cancer Rising is haunted by Doubt. This doubt manifests as a rejection of one's own intuitive guidance. The more she swims away from her primal impulses, the stronger the "psychic whirlpool" becomes. When she is held hostage by her own depths, she must call upon the Dragon to provide the ferocity needed to rise again. Just as mothers have been

---

1. R. H. Charles, *The Book of Enoch*, trans. R. H. Charles, intro. W. O. E. Oesterley (London: Society for Promoting Christian Knowledge, 1917), 77.

known to perform impossible feats of strength to save their children, this inner fountain of power is accessible to Cancer Rising the moment she grows past the fear of her own magnitude. This is **dragon consciousness:** the sacred pivot from being a victim of the tides to becoming the source of the tides.

INTEGRATION

The character of the Oracle—the Pythoness of Delphi—exemplifies the ghost of the Storyteller. Inhaling psychedelic vapors, she gave voice to primal truths that others had to interpret. The Oracle is the one who speaks the "unspoken." In the myth, it is the Oracle's words that haunt the characters. When Cancer Rising's inner Pythoness speaks, she must interpret the message from a place of faith.

Jocasta tried to escape the story rather than grapple with its meaning, wishing to keep her son in the dark even unto her death,

> *"O child of woe, I pray God, I pray God, thou never know!"*[2]

The ghost of the Storyteller reveals that beyond the duality of right and wrong, there is a "middle passage"—a place of chance and "*perhaps*" where the instinctive mind finally finds its voice. If Cancer Rising integrates the Storyteller, she learns to move with the twists and turns of the psyche, swimming like a serpent toward unexpected wisdom. She realizes that behind the Caretaker stands a dragon capable of making the impossible possible.

SUMMARY: The flow of a river is directed by the dragon that lives at its source.

---

2. Sophocles, *Oedipus King of Thebes*, trans. Gilbert Murray (London: George Allen & Unwin Ltd., 1911), 63.

5

LEO RISING: MASK OF THE MONARCH

Associated Archetypes: The Child, The Performer
Planetary Ruler: The Sun | **Element:** Fire | **Mode:** Fixed
Leo Rising is the pathway to: SELF-EXPRESSION
Ghost Sign: CANCER
Behind the Mask of THE MONARCH is the Ghost of THE CARETAKER
Leo Rising is haunted by: OBSCURITY
Fear Response: Inflation, exaggeration, and tyranny.
The Encrypted Wisdom: FEELINGS AND EMOTIONS
Integration: When responding from a place of vulnerability and authenticity, Leo Rising not only shines but also illuminates those around them.
Key Concept: Primal Purity

GHOSTLY ENCOUNTER

The masses gather at the palace gates. They brave the bitter cold to glimpse their king—a living symbol of dignity, prosperity, and hope. When he steps out onto the balcony, he radiates with the luminosity of a thousand suns. As distant as he appears to be, there is no one closer to the people than he. The Monarch has complete command of the moment. He lives from the center of the heart and serves as a bridge between the human and the divine. In return, he receives the well-deserved adoration of the world.

But the ghost of the Caretaker stands in the king's inner chamber. Her face is wet with tears; her lids are heavy with sorrow. Pressed against her breast is a child sucking the life out of her. This ghost cries to be seen, to be heard, and to be acknowledged. To hide this "unsightly" specter, the Monarch imprisons her in the deepest dungeon within his keep. As he loses touch with his heart, he loses touch with his people, and finally, with reality itself. Where once stood a mighty king, now stands a petty tyrant making an idol of a pride that hides a tired, desperate human being.

The Caretaker teaches Leo Rising the importance of a heart-centered life. Although strength and majesty are worthy of celebration, it is vulnerability that makes us "real." Embracing the flaws of the human condition imbues success with worth and life with meaning. The Caretaker asks Leo Rising to honor those "unsightly" emotions and to embrace his role as a living expression of the divine will.

NOTES FROM THE UNDERWORLD: PENTHEUS

King Pentheus of Thebes attempted to suppress the growing cult of Dionysus, feeling threatened by the god's chaotic power. Dionysus, appearing weak and captive, effortlessly escaped Pentheus's shackles and manipulated the king's own curiosity. He convinced Pentheus to spy on the sacred, ecstatic rites of the Theban women while disguised in women's clothing.

Upon discovering the intruder, the women—lost in a divine trance—attacked. Pentheus's own mother, Agave, led the charge, tearing her son limb from limb. Upon regaining her senses, Agave was devastated by the carnage of her actions.

SIGNS AND SYMBOLS

For ages, the lion has served as a symbol of power and majesty. The ancient kings of the Near East adorned their gateways with lions as guardians. James Hillman cites a tradition stating that lions were believed to be stillborn and had to be awakened to life by a roar.[1] This "roar" is the Leo Rising path; it is through the voice that one invigorates and awakens the dignity within the human heart.

As the Sun leaves the reflective season of Cancer, it moves into the joyous season of Leo—the summer's last act. The Sun is Leo's planetary ruler and is associated with the psychological process of individuation and the "royal road" to the true self. Leo rules the Fifth House—the House of Children—dealing with creativity, romance, and play. Leo Rising is here *to be* and *to become*, and through that radiance, they illuminate the world.

GHOSTLY DYNAMIC

In the myth of Pentheus, the king represents the mask of the Monarch, while his mother, Agave, represents the ghost of the Caretaker. The tragedy is one of un-acknowledgment. As Dionysus points out, the name *Pentheus* means "Man of Sorrow." His fate is foreshadowed: the more he rejects the divine, the more he rejects himself. By the end, he is no longer a king, but a fool in a disguise he cannot inhabit. His dying words to his mother go unheard as he is destroyed,

> *"Please recognize me."*[2]

When the ghost of the Caretaker is unintegrated, Leo Rising is haunted by Obscurity. From the Latin *obscurus*, meaning "dark" or "concealed," obscurity is the state of being unimportant or unknown.

---

1. James Hillman, "The Thought of the Heart," in *Facing the Gods*, ed. James Hillman (Irving, TX: Spring Publications, 1980), 52.
2. Euripides, *The Bacchae*, trans. E.S. Vellacott (London: Penguin Classics, 1954), 191.

When the heart is obscured, the individual becomes the *"bad actor"*—engaging in harmful behavior because they have lost their anchor. For Leo Rising, being obscure isn't just about fame; it's about the soul's light being concealed. Attributed to the French Queen, Marie Antoinette, is the quote, "Let them eat cake"—a phrase which highlights the cruelty those in power are capable of when the heart is obscured.

INTEGRATION

In the Christian tradition, Jesus noted that one must become "like a little child" to enter the kingdom of heaven. This is **primal purity**— a state where mortals speak with gods and the universe has complete access to itself. [3] This was the original understanding of kingship: a direct connection to the divine. Integration begins when the Monarch realizes that the throne is not a place to hide behind, but a seat of radical transparency. Once this realization occurs, the wisdom of feelings and emotions transforms a *"bad actor"* into an authentic presence.

The Lion is the perfect symbol for Leo because it takes the ferocity of a lion to defend the wildness of the inner child. In Asian temples, stone lions guard the entrance to remind visitors they are entering sacred ground. The ghost of the Caretaker teaches Leo Rising attunement; without a connection to one's own heart, one is not worthy of entering the sacred space of being. "*Living in Truth*" was an honorary title of the Great Egyptian Pharaoh, Akhenaten, and it serves as the compass for this path.

SUMMARY: Cowards and heroes are separated by a lion's roar.

3. Bancroft, *Origins of the Sacred*, 21.

6

VIRGO RISING: MASK OF THE SERVANT

Associated Archetypes: The Craftsperson, The Martyr
Planetary Ruler: Mercury | **Element:** Earth | **Mode:** Mutable
Virgo Rising is the pathway to: DISCERNMENT
Ghost Sign: LEO
Behind the Mask of THE SERVANT is the Ghost of THE MONARCH
Virgo Rising is haunted by: PERFECTION
Fear Response: Impossible standards leading to disappointment and despair.
The Encrypted Wisdom: SELF-EXPRESSION
Integration: Self-expression shatters the prison of perceived perfection, allowing the golden, illumined true self to be revealed.
Key Concept: Inscendence

GHOSTLY ENCOUNTER

The Servant feeds another branch into the temple fire. She approaches her task with the utmost severity; if that fire dies, her punishment is death. Always going above and beyond, she gives all of herself—mind, body, and soul. Those with eyes to see know that it is she who is the true temple flame.

But the ghost of the Monarch emerges from the shadows, offering the promise of perfection. Because of the Servant's fixation on the ideal, the real always seems to fall short. This schism between what is and what could be breeds a creeping dissatisfaction that, if left unchecked, collapses into a state of chronic neurosis. When she succumbs to impossible expectations, her inner Monarch becomes a tyrant and a tormentor. She who was the guardian of the fire becomes the sacrificial lamb, slaughtered on the altar of the unattainable.

The relentless quest for perfection is a maze with no exit; only through authentic self-expression does she find her freedom. The Servant must ask herself a vital question: "Who, or what, am I in service to?" The Monarch teaches Virgo Rising to embrace the beautiful mess of human nature. Perfection is not a destination to be reached; it is a guiding star leading us toward the mystery that lies beyond.

NOTES FROM THE UNDERWORLD: IPHIGENIA

On his way to the Trojan War, King Agamemnon killed a sacred stag belonging to Artemis. The goddess of the wild took great offense, halting the Greek fleet with unfavorable winds. To appease her, the seer Calchas declared that the King must sacrifice his daughter, Iphigenia. Agamemnon lured her to the port of Aulis with a lie, promising her she was to be wed to the hero Achilles.

When Iphigenia arrived and learned the grim truth, she begged for her life, but ultimately accepted her doom for the sake of the mission. In one version of the myth, she is slaughtered. In another, Artemis—moved by the girl's purity—substitutes a deer at the final moment, whisking Iphigenia away to serve as a priestess in her temple.

SIGNS AND SYMBOLS

Discernment is the "ability to judge well." In mystical traditions, it is a spiritual gift—the capacity to grasp what is obscure. This is Virgoan energy: alert, vigilant, and acute in its judgment because everything is on the line. This level of attention is a form of reverence. The Cherokee believed a hunter only killed a deer because the animal chose to reveal itself, deeming the hunter "worthy" of its sacrifice. To the Cherokee, the hunt was a dialogue of mutual respect. This is the core of Virgo: to be in worthy service, where the quality of one's attention determines the sanctity of the work.

The Sun's entry into Virgo marks the start of Autumn and the labor-intensive harvest. Here, the Mercurial energy that was "everywhere at all at once" in Gemini becomes direct and precise. This focus is best expressed in the archetype of the Craftsperson, who uses the discipline of the body to channel chaotic energy into functional grace. Virgo rules the Sixth House—the House of Servants—encompassing routine, skill, health, and work. It is Virgo Rising's devotion to her labor that makes her the "midwife of the miraculous."

GHOSTLY DYNAMIC

The shadow dynamic at play is the *royal promise*, where the ghostly Monarch offers the Servant mask an ideal that does not exist. We see this in Agamemnon's promise of "perfect union," a lie that mirrors the Fall of Eve. When the serpent suggested, *"Eat of this fruit and you shall become like God,"* the promise served as a catalyst for the soul's descent from the anesthesia of paradise into the jagged reality of consciousness.

Such a fall is not a failure, but a necessary evolution. The *royal promise* of perfection provides the essential friction that forces the soul out of the ideal and into the material world. It is through this loss of innocence that true wisdom is born; Iphigenia only truly knows the divine when the *royal promise* is revealed as a lie. Similarly, it is only after a fall that the seeker gains sovereign knowledge of their own nature.

In the polarity of Pisces, spirituality is transcendence—rising above. In Virgo, it is **inscendence.** Coined by cultural historian and theologian Thomas Berry, **inscendence** is the impulse to crawl into the world and seek its core.[1] For Virgo Rising, spirituality is not something to rise toward; it is something to fall into.

INTEGRATION

The transition from the ideal to the real is the point of Crisis. Stemming from the Greek *krísi*, it means a "turning point" indicating either recovery or death. A crisis is a cosmic opportunity for the true self to emerge. In Jungian thought, the experience of the Self is always a "defeat" for the ego.

Humility—a word whose root *humus* means "close to the earth"—is the quality that keeps Virgo Rising coherent. She must journey from the serpent's lie to the serpent's wisdom, leaving behind assumptions of how things should be to embrace the beauty of how things are. By grounding herself in this truth, she finds the courage for authentic self-expression; she no longer performs a role of perfection, but instead reveals the golden reality of her own being.

This is beautifully illustrated by Kintsugi, the Japanese art of mending broken ceramics with gold. By highlighting the cracks rather than hiding them, this tradition celebrates the object's history. For Virgo Rising, it is through the flaws and the brokenness that the light of the soul finds expression. As Rumi wrote: *"You have to keep breaking your heart until it opens."*

SUMMARY: The serpent speaks the truth, but only if you're willing to fall for it.

1. Thomas Berry, *The Dream of the Earth* (San Francisco: Sierra Club Books, 1988), 208.

7

LIBRA RISING: MASK OF THE LOVER

Associated Archetypes: The Artist, The Diplomat
Planetary Ruler: Venus | **Element:** Air | **Mode:** Cardinal
Libra Rising is the pathway to: PARTNERSHIP
Ghost Sign: VIRGO
Behind the Mask of THE LOVER is the Ghost of THE SERVANT
Libra Rising is haunted by: INDECISION
Fear Response: Maintaining a "false peace" at the expense of personal growth and development.
The Encrypted Wisdom: DISCERNMENT
Integration: The ability to make heart-centered judgments and take decisive actions which result in genuine relationships.
Key Concept: Mirroring

GHOSTLY ENCOUNTER

Beneath the cherry blossom lies the Lover. Against the backdrop of a blue sky, pink petals rain down from the branches above. He opens his palm and catches one; he knows that within the petal lies a poem. This gesture expresses his innate ability to grasp the poetry in all things, to see every side of a story, and to embrace the paradoxical nature of reality. But something is missing. The Lover yearns for his magical other, for he knows it is through partnership that he finds the balance he desires. If beauty is a song, it is the Lover who strikes the chords.

In the Lover's garden, however, lurks the ghost of the Servant. She slithers between the hedges, her eyes as piercing as daggers, her fingers splayed like the talons of a raptor eager to seize its prey. To keep the peace, the Lover avoids her horrid gaze. He takes refuge in a state of indecision, believing that making no move is better than making the wrong move. Stagnation replaces action; posturing overcomes authentic expression; superficiality replaces depth. Without realizing it, the Lover falls victim to the Gorgon's gaze. Where once stood the Lover, there now stands a living statue—mute and motionless—watching as the world passes him by.

The ghost of the Servant teaches the fine art of Discernment, which means "to separate." This is the great paradox of the Lover's path: he who yearns for partnership must first learn separation. It is through discernment that the Lover makes the choices necessary to support the evolving soul. When the Lover grasps the Servant's teachings, he has a priceless gift to offer: himself—genuine, confident, and a true work of art.

NOTES FROM THE UNDERWORLD: THE PHANTOM HELEN

Helen of Sparta, the most beautiful woman on earth, is legendary for the war her elopement ignited. However, a contrasting narrative by Euripides suggests a different fate: Helen never reached Troy. Instead, the gods spirited her away to Egypt, leaving behind an *eidolon*—a phantom double—to take her place. While the "Phantom Helen" lived in Troy and fueled a ten-year war, the real Helen remained in Egypt, faithful to her husband Menelaus and resisting all suitors.

Following the war, a shipwrecked Menelaus arrived in Egypt, carrying the phantom he had "rescued" from Troy. He could not distinguish between the two until the phantom suddenly vanished into thin air. Their reunion led to a clever ruse where Helen, feigning grief, tricked her Egyptian suitor into providing a ship for a ritual burial at sea, allowing the couple to escape back to Greece.

SIGNS AND SYMBOLS

In the human experience, the encounter with the phantom self begins before the mirror. But this reflection extends far beyond the physical glass; it manifests as the psychological phenomenon of **Mirroring**—the unconscious imitation of gestures that builds the bridge of rapport between two souls.[1] By literally "seeing" ourselves in the movements and emotions of another, we move from isolation to empathy. This recognition of the self in the *Other* is the spiritual foundation of Justice and the essential heartbeat of a civilized society.

The Autumnal Equinox marks the season of Libra, a time when light and dark find temporary balance. Nature turns up the dial on her allure, displaying stunning hues of red and gold. Libra rules the Seventh House—the House of Marriage. Positioned opposite Aries (the House of Self), it suggests that we gain an expansive perspective of ourselves through our relationships with others.

Venus, the ruler of Libra, expresses her energy here through tension and abstraction. To create, the Artist must be close to the work, yet step back to gain perspective. While the mirror can symbolize vanity, it is primarily a symbol of the bridge between Self and Other.

GHOSTLY DYNAMIC

In our analysis, the real Helen represents the mask of the Lover, while the phantom Helen of Troy represents the ghost of the Servant. The Greeks called such a phantom an *eidolon* (εἴδωλον)—a specter or

1. Tanya L. Chartrand and John A. Bargh, "The Chameleon Effect: The Perception-Behavior Link and Social Interaction," *Journal of Personality and Social Psychology* 76 (1999): 893–910.

an "image of a god." An *eidolon* is an ideal; it appears in the world but has no substance. It is a potential without a pulse.

Regarding Helen, the Elizabethan playwright Christopher Marlowe famously asked, "*Is this the face that launch'd a thousand ships?*" In our analysis, this question reveals the shadow of Libra Rising who clings to the ideal at the cost of a genuine relationship. Like the phantom Helen, he remains a face without a body—a spectator to his own existence. Safe behind the high walls of Troy, he is shielded from the blood, sweat, and tears that irrigate a meaningful life. Without the courage to be "messy," he becomes a magnificent statue: beautiful to behold, but incapable of the living warmth that only true vulnerability provides.

INTEGRATION

The ghost of the Servant carries the wisdom of Discernment. The etymology of discernment—from the Latin *discernere*—reminds us that the Lover's path requires the courage to sort the real from the phantom. In order for Libra Rising to be in genuine relationship, the wisdom of separation is necessary. This paradox is also present in the Libran concept of "reflection," which means an image double, but is also used to describe a solitary process of serious thought and consideration.

For Libra Rising, the art is to stay open and sensitive while remaining steadfast in holding the space between Self and Other. While the desire for belonging is profound, true wisdom lies in the discernment to judge the quality of one's alliances. Peace and harmony do not come from a lack of conflict, but through strength and pursuit of virtue.

SUMMARY: The world is your mirror; make yourself beautiful, and your reflection will follow.

8

SCORPIO RISING: MASK OF THE INVESTIGATOR

Associated Archetypes: The Shaman, The Secret Agent
Planetary Ruler: Mars and Pluto | **Element:** Water | **Mode:** Fixed
Scorpio Rising is the pathway to: TRANSFORMATION
Ghost Sign: LIBRA
Behind the Mask of THE INVESTIGATOR is the Ghost of THE LOVER
Scorpio Rising is haunted by: BETRAYAL
Fear Response: Obsession, compulsion, aggression, and self-destruction.
The Encrypted Wisdom: PARTNERSHIP
Integration: Genuine and healthy relationships grant access to unimaginable psychic depths and transformative powers.
Key Concept: The Healing Poison

GHOSTLY ENCOUNTER

From the shadows, the Investigator watches with an eagle eye. She penetrates the unseen and unspoken depths of the human psyche, expertly disguising herself to achieve her goals. As one fluent in the language of shadows, she allows little to remain hidden. It is through fire she dies, and through fire she is reborn. She is the Phoenix, the breath of the Dragon, and the agent of transformation.

Beneath the Investigator's aura of intensity and sexual magnetism lies a wound of betrayal. In the center of this wound resides the ghost of the Lover. His song is a haunting melody of lost harmony and broken promises, drawing the Investigator deeper into the dark. If his song mesmerizes her, she takes up permanent residence in a psychic space where every choice is informed by the pain of the past. Hell becomes a state of being.

When the principle of partnership is integrated, Scorpio Rising gains the ability to view her own depths without being swallowed by them. The Libran mirror provides perspective, helping her move beyond obsessive fixation and into a realm of action defined by intention. The ghost of the Lover teaches Scorpio Rising a hard truth: she finds herself only by letting go of herself.

NOTES FROM THE UNDERWORLD: MEDEA

Medea, the great enchantress of Greek mythology, was a descendant of Gods who possessed the gift of prophecy and magic. The philosopher Apollonius called her a *polypharmakos* (πολυφάρμακος), from the Greek *pharmakon* (φάρμακον), meaning both "medicine" and "poison." This duality encompassed the knowledge of the alchemical preparations of herbs and their magical effects.

Medea used her *pharmaka* throughout her mythos: she rendered Jason impervious to flame using a potion grown from the blood of Prometheus and resurrected the dead. Yet, she also used her poisons to kill Jason's new bride and her own children. Medea's poison, as both life-giver and death-dealer, exemplifies the core duality of the Scorpionic path: that which has the power to destroy also holds the power to redeem.

SIGNS AND SYMBOLS

The concept of the *pharmakon,* or the **healing poison** is the key to Scorpio Rising. Beyond potions, the *pharmakos* was also a ritual where scapegoats were expelled from a community to banish evil. This reflects the Scorpionic process: purification via fire. The mystic Meister Eckhart captured this Scorpionic process in his teachings on detachment: To the soul that clings, this fire is a tormentor; to the soul that surrenders, it is the agent of liberation.

Scorpio season marks the time when darkness overcomes light. Halloween, rooted in the Celtic Samhain, honors the moment when the veil between the living and the dead is thinnest. Traditional ruler Mars oversees the development of the will, while modern ruler Pluto governs the soul's capacity to journey into the realms of depth, meaning, and transformation. Scorpio rules the Eighth House—the House of Death, which deals with themes of death, sexuality, psychological truth, other people's resources, and the taboo. This is where the fires of hell are revealed to be the heat of a divine kiln; they do not exist to destroy the soul, but to burn away the dross of the ego.

GHOSTLY DYNAMIC

Caught in the tension between the mask of the Investigator and the ghost of the Lover is the figure of Medea. Evident in her character arc is a brutal Scorpionic law: to honor her own soul, she must betray another. To access the wisdom of partnership, Scorpio Rising must reckon with this ghost of betrayal—the understanding that intimacy and sacrifice are often one and the same.

The word betrayal comes from the Latin *tradere*, meaning to "hand over." This archetypal "handing over" is echoed in the story of Judas. Occult investigator Jordan Maxwell connected the "Judas kiss" to Scorpionic symbolism, noting that the kiss used to identify the victim mirrors the two small, kiss-like punctures left by a scorpion's sting. If we view the story of Jesus as a solar myth, this betrayal represents the sun's descent in Scorpio as it enters the darkness of winter.

This ritual mark is further echoed in the *il bacio della morte* of the Mafioso, a kiss used by bosses to mark a member for death following a perceived betrayal. For the Scorpio Rising, these narratives reveal an uncomfortable occult truth: the kiss of love and the kiss of death are two sides of the same coin. Like Medea, she must decide if this realization will destroy her, or set her free.

INTEGRATION

The Gnostic gospels suggest Judas was the most cherished disciple, entrusted with a singular mystery. Jesus told him,

> "You will sacrifice the man that clothes me." [1]

To betray the "man that clothes me," the ego or the persona—is the essential Scorpionic task. Just as Medea only ascends on her chariot of golden serpents after betraying her worldly roles, Scorpio Rising finds liberation by sacrificing the habits and identities she holds dearest. This is the "Harrowing of Hell," where the divine descends into the abyss not as punishment, but as a rescue mission for the soul. To redeem ourselves, we must first have the courage to meet our shadows in the dark.

Esoterically, while the Scorpion crawls in the sand, its higher symbol of the White Eagle soars in the sky.[2] Somewhere between the desert and the heavens, Scorpio Rising masters the ultimate lesson: to truly love is to be able to let go.

SUMMARY: Where stands a divine presence inviting one into her loving embrace, there also is cast the shadow of death.

1. Bart D. Ehrman, *The Lost Gospel of Judas Iscariot: A New Look at Betrayer and Betrayed* (Oxford: Oxford University Press, 2006), 88.
2. George W. Carey and Inez Eudora Perry, The *Zodiac and the Salts of Salvation* (Hollywood, CA: The Carey-Perry School of the Chemistry of Life, 1932), 222.

9

SAGITTARIUS RISING: MASK OF THE PHILOSOPHER

Associated Archetypes: The Gypsy, The Scholar
Planetary Ruler: Jupiter | **Element:** Fire | **Mode:** Mutable
Sagittarius Rising is the pathway to: DIRECTION
Ghost Sign: SCORPIO
Behind the Mask of THE PHILOSOPHER is the Ghost of THE INVESTIGATOR
Sagittarius Rising is haunted by: STAGNATION
Fear Response: Rigid beliefs and reckless "leaps of faith" that crush everything in their path.
The Encrypted Wisdom: TRANSFORMATION
Integration: When the Philosopher looks into the dark sockets of the human skull, he directs his questions toward the wisdom he seeks.
Key Concept: Serpent Wisdom

GHOSTLY ENCOUNTER

Relentless in his pursuit of truth, who is this man of wisdom? He battles alongside heroes, drinks with centaurs, and wrestles with gods. He is the Philosopher: a true seeker whose beliefs stem not from blind faith, but from real-world experience. He believes because he *knows*. To the Philosopher, borders are not boundaries but invitations to explore what lies beyond.

However, our wandering Philosopher travels with a phantom companion: the ghost of the Investigator. Her crooked finger points to a corpse by the road. While the Philosopher tries to outrun the image of death, the image of death cannot let go of him. If he has not made peace with his Scorpionic ghost, he experiences life's inevitable transformations as an enemy seeking to clip his wings. He responds with urgency and recklessness. Where once stood a Philosopher, now stands a gambler risking it all in a loser's game.

The ghost of the Investigator teaches the Philosopher profound truths concerning death and change. By integrating this shadow, he becomes more strategic and intentional. In the wisdom of death, he finds the key to rebirth. Like a serpent, he learns to shed his skin—letting go of limiting beliefs and dogmatic worldviews. This allows him to be reborn into more expansive states of being.

NOTES FROM THE UNDERWORLD: PIRITHOUS

Pirithous, King of the Lapiths, was famed for his reckless ambition. He aimed to wed a divine bride: Persephone, Queen of the Underworld and wife of Hades. Despite the cautions of his friend Theseus, Pirithous ventured into the shadowy realm, fueled by mortal hubris. Hades, aware of the plan, feigned hospitality, offering them seats at a banquet. But these were the Chairs of Forgetfulness, and they bound the heroes, rooting their bodies to stone.

Later, Heracles discovered them. He successfully freed Theseus, but when he attempted to liberate Pirithous, the earth shuddered with Hades' wrath. Pirithous, his arrogance deemed beyond redemption, remained imprisoned—a stark reminder of the consequences of seeking "higher" truths while disrespecting the "lower" depths.

SIGNS AND SYMBOLS

The primary symbol of this path is the centauric archer, a creature of dual nature. Above the waist, he is human, representing the light of reason and inquiry; below, he is a horse, symbolizing the wild, instinctual drive of the animal body.[1] Such a fusion is essential to the quest for truth, for without a clear aim to unify these two halves, the Sagittarius archetype remains undirected energy—a race without a destination.

Sagittarius season marks the arrival of winter, bringing people around fires to share adventurous tales and contemplate life's profound questions. This mirrors Jupiter's influence, which fosters faith and confidence. Sagittarius governs the Ninth House—the House of Long Journeys Over Water—encompassing foreign encounters, higher education, and ethics. Here, we are urged to transcend outdated routines. Encounters with the external "foreign" lead us to discover the internal "foreign," yielding the gold of profound wisdom.

GHOSTLY DYNAMIC

In the architectural tension between the Philosopher mask and the Investigator ghost, we find the hubris of Pirithous. In the ancient language of archery, *missing the mark* was the original definition of the word *sin* (ἁμαρτία). For Sagittarius Rising, this "sin" occurs when they lose sight of the horizon and attempt to outrun the very transformations their soul demands.

In this mythic landscape, Pirithous serves as the Philosopher who has lost his aim, blinded by an arrogance that eventually roots him to the "Chair of Forgetfulness." Conversely, Hercules exemplifies the Scorpionic depths the Archer must integrate to find his mark. Before descending to retrieve Cerberus, Hercules did not storm the gates; he

---

1. Ariel Guttman and Kenneth Johnson, *Mythic Astrology* (St. Paul, MN: Llewellyn Publications, 1993), 324.

underwent initiation into the mysteries, approaching the underworld with reverence rather than the bargaining of a gambler. By freeing Theseus but leaving the hubristic Pirithous behind, Hercules demonstrates the discernment of the depths. He recognizes that some stagnations are the result of moral transgression—and it is this recognition of one's own fallibility that allows the Philosopher to navigate the abyss without being swallowed by it.

INTEGRATION

The ghost of the Investigator holds the key to Transformation. In the Sumerian myth of *Inanna*, she must surrender her scepter, jewelry, and clothing to approach the throne of the Underworld queen "naked and bowed low."[2] To approach mystery, one must be willing to surrender the authority of the ego.

Just as a serpent becomes naked by shedding its skin to grow, the Sagittarius Rising must re-evaluate his beliefs and appetites. Truth is not something to be grasped, but something to move toward. This is the **serpent wisdom** offered by Scorpio in the Twelfth House: the ability to "die" to an old identity to be reborn into a deeper state of consciousness.

SUMMARY: You are not going anywhere unless you leave something behind.

2. Diane Wolkstein, *Inanna, Queen of Heaven and Earth: Her Stories and Hymns from Sumer* (New York: Harper & Row, 1983), 158.

10

CAPRICORN RISING: MASK OF THE ELDER

Associated Archetypes: The Architect, The Hermit
Planetary Ruler: Saturn | **Element:** Earth | **Mode:** Cardinal
Capricorn Rising is the pathway to: REALIZATION
Ghost Sign: SAGITTARIUS
Behind the Mask of THE ELDER is the Ghost of THE PHILOSOPHER
Capricorn Rising is haunted by: AIMLESSNESS
Fear Response: Ruthless ambition and self-imposed restrictions resulting in deep isolation.
The Encrypted Wisdom: DIRECTION
Integration: When Capricorn Rising aligns action with honor and responsibility with morality, she reaches a state of integrity.
Key Concept: A Deal with the Devil

GHOSTLY ENCOUNTER

Civilization has plunged into despair. The noble institutions that once protected humanity crumble like castles of sand. When all else fails, the people turn to the Elder. With her natural sense of leadership and ability to shoulder tremendous burdens, she carries humanity through the hardest of times. She is the emblem of maturity, dignity, and integrity. Time spent in solitude, and the reflection it provides, is her greatest asset.

Yet, the ghost of the Philosopher appears like a dark angel on the mountaintop. He speaks the language of "unlimited growth" and "shortcuts to the stars," promising riches and power without the toll of time. If Capricorn Rising makes this "deal with the devil," attaining prestige by sacrificing her soul, she loses her path. Devoured by her ambitions, her success becomes her prison cell, and her sentence is life in solitary confinement.

Integrity is the keyword. Her strength comes from the very bonds and structures that may seem limiting. The Philosopher's offer is a test: Capricorn Rising must stay true to herself to fulfill the work she was born to realize. If successful, she stands as a living testimony to tradition, acting as a pathfinder for a humanity that has forgotten the way.

NOTES FROM THE UNDERWORLD: TANTALUS

Tantalus, a king and progenitor of a cursed lineage, incurred the gods' wrath through his wicked deeds. As the son of Zeus, he enjoyed the privilege of feasting with the gods—a favor he abused. His most notorious act was a test of divine omniscience: he murdered his son, Pelops, and served him as a stew to the gods, believing he could expose their ignorance.

The gods recognized the horrific truth and banished Tantalus to the deepest regions of the underworld. His punishment was eternal frustration: standing in a pool of water beneath fruit-laden branches. Whenever he reached for fruit, the branches rose; whenever he bent to drink, the water receded. He became a prisoner of his own greed, forever denied the nourishment he craved.

SIGNS AND SYMBOLS

Maturity is defined as a "very developed or advanced state," symbolized primarily by the Saturnian Ring. This boundary encompasses the sacred union of the wedding (the wedding ring), the rigorous testing of the wrestling match (the wrestling ring), and even the clown's folly (the circus ring). To cross the bridge into adulthood, one must pay a toll to Lord Saturn, who stands as the guardian of the gate. The ring serves as a permanent reminder that we are subject to the laws of time and space; it is only by stepping into "the ring" that an individual is finally made real.

The Winter Solstice, the shortest day and longest night, defines Capricorn season. Darkness is at its peak, yet it is here the light shines brightest. Planetary ruler Saturn oversees the development of discipline, self-respect, and the brick walls of reality. The Greeks knew him as *Cronos*, who in his light aspect ruled the Golden Age of prosperity, and in his dark aspect is the reaper come to separate the wheat from the chaff. Capricorn rules the highest point in the natal chart, the Tenth House, the House of Career. This house is associated with public image, authority, leadership, and legacy.

GHOSTLY DYNAMIC

In the psychodrama of Capricorn Rising, the figure of Tantalus serves as a warning as to what happens when the Elder fails to integrate his Philosopher ghost. Though Tantalus was granted a seat at the table of the gods, he lacked the integrity to remain there. Plato noted that the name *Tantalus* (Τάνταλος) means "one who has to bear much,"[1] a title that foreshadows the heavy burden of those who seek to bypass the laws of the spirit to satisfy the hungers of the ego.

With Sagittarius in the Twelfth House, the natural sense of faith, hope, and optimism is obscured, making the Philosopher-Ghost's

1. Plato, "Cratylus," in *The Dialogues of Plato*, trans. Benjamin Jowett (New York and London: Macmillan and Co., 1892), 338.

offer of a "shortcut" to the top nearly irresistible. In this shadow state, the ghost acts as the Tempter, promising relief from the arduous climb if only the Capricorn rising will compromise her values. Just as Tantalus sacrificed his son to prove a point, the unintegrated Capricorn Rising sacrifices her own "Sun"—her inner vitality, warmth, bonds, and connections—to secure a cold and lonely prestige. It is a **deal with the devil.**

The dual predicament of Capricorn Rising is to be called to the holy peaks while being tested by the gravity of her own ambition. She must remember that her totem is not merely a goat, but the Sea-Goat. To reach the summit without losing her soul, she cannot climb as a dry, rigid shell; she must bring the living waters of the deep up the mountain with her.

INTEGRATION

To grasp the wisdom of Direction, Capricorn Rising must engage the ghost of the Philosopher. In the Zen tradition of archery, the archer is both the aimer and the aim.[2] This is Integrity—the state of being whole and undivided. Work and status must become reflections of an inner truth.

Upholding integrity mirrors the creation of a diamond, formed under immense pressure. In Buddhism, the diamond metaphor represents the ability to cut through illusion. The *Diamond Sutra* reminds us that this fleeting world is like "a star at dawn, a bubble in a stream." By acknowledging the transient nature of status, the Elder finds the direction required to build something that truly lasts.

SUMMARY: The beauty of what is, is oftentimes built on the sorrow of what could have been.

2. Eugen Herrigel, *Zen in the Art of Archery* (New York: Pantheon Books, 1953), 6.

11

AQUARIUS RISING: MASK OF THE OUTLAW

Associated Archetypes: The Genius, The Revolutionary
Planetary Ruler: Uranus and Saturn | **Element:** Air | **Mode:** Fixed
Aquarius Rising is the pathway to: DISTRIBUTION
Ghost Sign: CAPRICORN
Behind the Mask of THE OUTLAW is the Ghost of THE ELDER
Aquarius Rising is haunted by: CONFORMITY
Fear Response: Lofty ideals, stifled genius, and a spirit that leads to alienation.
The Encrypted Wisdom: REALIZATION
Integration: Developing the ability to create structures that bring genius out of the ideal and into the real, connected and in service to humanity.
Key Concept: The Third Way

GHOSTLY ENCOUNTER

An angry crowd gathers in the town square, the scent of burning wood thick in the air. At the center of the uproar, tied to a stake, is the Outlaw. As the flames rise, he gazes at the rabid mob and flashes a smile. With his final breath, he shocks the world by defying its expectations. His crime? Radical authenticity. As time passes, his "heresies" are validated and "the righteous" are exposed.

Haunting the Outlaw is the ghost of the Elder. Like a cross upon the Outlaw's back, the Elder applies constant pressure. This time-tested wisdom can feel like a crushing weight, jeopardizing the pursuit of absolute freedom. Yet, to liberate his genius, the Outlaw needs the Elder's gravity. Without it, his ideas never land; they hover like a UFO, beaming him up and off the earth. No longer a revolutionary, he becomes alienated—disconnected from humanity and himself.

While the Outlaw provides vision, the Elder possesses the wisdom to make it real. Symbolizing Realization, the Elder's cross provides the tension required to pull potential into manifestation. Having survived life's trials, the Elder offers the Outlaw the most extraordinary gift: shoulders to stand on.

NOTES FROM THE UNDERWORLD: IXION

Ixion (Ἰξίων), King of the Lapiths, stands as one of Greek mythology's most notorious tricksters. To evade paying a bride price, he resorted to murder, a violation of the sacred law of hospitality. Because he was the first mortal to slay a blood relative, his countrymen refused him purification. Driven to madness, he became a fugitive until Zeus, in an act of benevolence, invited him to Olympus.

Ungrateful for this second chance, Ixion attempted to seduce Zeus's wife, Hera. To confirm the betrayal, Zeus crafted a cloud-double of Hera named Nephele (Νεφέλη). Deceived, Ixion lay with the phantom and later boasted of conquering a goddess. From this union, the race of centaurs was born. Enraged, Zeus struck Ixion with a thunderbolt and commanded Hermes to bind him to a fiery, eternally spinning wheel in the underworld.

SIGNS AND SYMBOLS

In the Gospel of Luke (22:10), Jesus gives a cryptic instruction:

> *"Behold, when ye are entered into the city, there shall a man meet you, bearing a pitcher of water; follow him into the house where he entereth in."*

In the ancient world, carrying water was a task exclusive to women—a biological echo of the amniotic fluid. The radical image of a *man* carrying water suggests a "breaking of the water" on a cosmic scale; many esotericists believe this was a nod to the coming Aquarian Age. Just as the breaking of the water precedes a birth, this symbol heralds the delivery of a new world. This associates Aquarius with the Scientist and the Revolutionary who must defy the established order to deliver a gift that transforms humanity.

Traditional ruler Saturn governs discipline and endurance, while modern ruler Uranus ignites radical authenticity and the capacity to question authority. Aquarius rules the Eleventh House—the House of Friends and Good Spirits. Historically, planets here were considered in "clear vision," liberated from the captivity of the Twelfth House. While the Tenth House represents the culmination of a career, the Eleventh represents the aspiration toward a more elevated state.[1] Aquarius Rising sparks the revolution that leads to evolution.

GHOSTLY DYNAMIC

In the mythic psychodrama of Aquarius Rising, Ixion represents the mask of the Outlaw, while Zeus acts as the ghost of the Elder. Ixion's downfall began when he became infatuated with *Nephele*—a cloud-nymph shaped in the image of a goddess, but possessing no substance. By disregarding the "Elder" wisdom of divine law to chase

---

1. Deborah Houlding, *The Houses, Temples of the Sky* (London: The Wessex Astrologer Ltd, 2006), 40.

this phantom, Ixion was sentenced to spin powerless on a fiery wheel for eternity.

This mythic warning echoes in our digital age, where the "Cloud" has become a vast repository of data—a realm of ideals often detached from the pulse of reality. For the Aquarius Rising, the challenge is to hold the electric tension between innovation (Uranus) and tradition (Saturn). Carl Jung believed that by reconciling these opposites, a **third way** emerges: genius unleashed. Without this balance, evolutionary potential collapses into a self-destructive cycle. Ixion's wheel is the ultimate Aquarian shadow: Alienation. It is the state of being held captive by one's own beautiful, but barren, phantoms.

INTEGRATION

Contrast Ixion's wheel with Leonardo da Vinci's *Vitruvian Man*. This image encapsulates the Renaissance ideal of humanism, placing humankind at the center of the universe. Here, the wheel is not a torture device; it is a frame that contains a man standing with purpose. Crucially, by reconciling the "Circle of Uranus" with the "Square of Saturn," the Vitruvian Man symbolizes a perfect harmony between the timeless heavens and time-based physical reality. This is Ixion redeemed—no longer a captive to the wheel, but a conduit for the divine.

The ghost of the Elder, having watched the wheel of time spin for eons, reminds Aquarius Rising that radical change requires a steady hand. For genius to be useful, it must be contained. This is the mystery of the **third way**: the realization that the "Circle" of infinite possibility can only be distributed to the world through the "Square" of structural reality.

SUMMARY: The power of a raindrop is revealed in the act of touching the earth.

12

PISCES RISING: MASK OF THE MYSTIC

Associated Archetypes: The Poet, The Dreamer
Planetary Ruler: Jupiter and Neptune | **Element:** Water | **Mode:** Mutable
Pisces Rising is the pathway to: TRANSCENDENCE
Ghost Sign: AQUARIUS
Behind the Mask of THE MYSTIC is the Ghost of THE OUTLAW
Pisces Rising is haunted by: ASSIMILATION
Fear Response: Addiction and escapism.
The Encrypted Wisdom: DISTRIBUTION
Integration: Embracing the genius in sensitivity, gaining access to meaningful states of transcendence that provide profound and mystical insight.
Key Concept: The Womb Realm

GHOSTLY ENCOUNTER

The Mystic sits by a stream, conversing with small birds. Her eyes are as deep as the sea, her nature ephemeral; no one can possess her. Like a dolphin, she leaps between the realms of dreaming and waking, delighting in the soul she feels permeating all things. Her selflessness is the root of her compassion and psychic attunement. When the gods whisper, it is the Mystic who hears.

However, such selflessness is a double-edged sword. The onslaught of external thoughts and feelings leaves her struggling to remain embodied. In her confusion, the ghost of the Outlaw appears with an escape plan. In his lower expression, he is a conman or a dealer offering a quick fix. Her nature is twisted, and she finds herself devoted to the rituals of addiction, living as a ghost in her own flesh. She soon realizes the hard lesson: beyond the mystical door lies an infinite sea of madness.

In his higher expression, the ghost of the Outlaw offers freedom instead of escape. He holds the gift of Genius—the tool needed to navigate psychic realms while remaining functional in the physical world. When the Mystic embraces this genius, existence is no longer a disaster to flee, but a dream made flesh.

NOTES FROM THE UNDERWORLD: PENELOPE

Homer's *Odyssey* tells of Penelope, Queen of Ithaca, who waited twenty years for her husband's return. Besieged by over a hundred suitors who consumed her resources and pressured her to remarry, Penelope devised a clever ruse. She claimed she must weave a death shroud for her father-in-law before choosing a husband. Each night, she secretly unraveled the day's work, keeping the task—and the suitors—at bay. Her story is a testament to the power of faith, patience, and the strategic "unweaving" of reality.

SIGNS AND SYMBOLS

The *Hieros Ichthys* (Sacred Fish) represents divine love, a symbol further enriched by the ancient Greek view of the Dolphin as a sacred guardian and guide. The word dolphin stems from *delphis*, related to *delphys*, meaning "womb."[1] This connects to Delphi, the "navel of the Earth," where the oracle offered cryptic divinations.

Like the dolphin, Pisces Rising moves between worlds with grace. Her path highlights the importance of dreaming, resting, and surrendering to the divine source. Pisces season marks the end of the astrological year, acting as a doorway to a new cycle. Traditional ruler Jupiter provides the necessary expansion of the heart, while modern ruler Neptune grants the vision required for the journey. Pisces governs the Twelfth House—the House of Self-Undoing. Historically a place of trouble, it is actually a porous boundary allowing passage into mystical realms. Transcendence requires the "unraveling" of the individual, laying down the life they think they have to live to embrace the great mystery.

GHOSTLY DYNAMIC

Caught in the crossfire between the mask of the Mystic and the Ghost of the Outlaw is the figure of Penelope. For an individual with extreme psychic sensitivity, the world can feel like a war zone. Like a flower crushed by a tank, the sensitive soul risks being assimilated into the environment, losing the distinction between "I" and "We." To cope, Pisces Rising often turns to escapism—misguided attempts to preserve psychic integrity.

When distorted, the Outlaw ghost appears as the "Mob"—the overpowering collective urges that lie beneath civilization. Odysseus described the suitors as rascals "*gorging themselves... with no rational end in sight.*"[2] To navigate this unspoken tyranny, Pisces Rising must learn that her sensitivity is not a burden to escape, but a genius to embrace.

---

1. Douglas Harper, "dolphin," *Online Etymology Dictionary*, accessed March 30, 2026.
2. Homer, *The Odyssey: Revised Prose Translation*, trans. E. V. Rieu (Harmondsworth: Penguin Books, 1946), 256.

INTEGRATION

The encrypted wisdom of the Twelfth House is the principle of Distribution—the act of sharing one's internal riches with the collective. For Pisces Rising, this genius manifests as the ability to unite with the divine Source while simultaneously distributing that light to others through overt acts like service and art, or covert acts such as prayer and dreaming. This is the "Third Way" of the Outlaw: refusing to be crushed by the world or to flee from it, but instead choosing to re-imagine it entirely.

Returning to the *Odyssey*, we can view Odysseus' journey through the water as a baptism, while Penelope acts as the Mystic who holds the sacred space for his rebirth. She does not run from the mob, nor does she surrender to it. Instead, she uses her Aquarian Genius to weave and unweave a reality that buys time for a miracle. She becomes a "Sky Dancer," much like the Buddhist *Dakini*—a figure who dances in the "sky'"of absolute emptiness.[3] Just as the Dakini represents the liberation found in the "Womb Realm," Penelope's unweaving reveals that true Transcendence is the ability to move through the world without being defined by its structures.

By embracing the Outlaw's genius, Pisces Rising no longer fears being lost in the sea of the collective. She becomes the living threshold between heaven and earth, securing the space for the old world to pass away and for a new world to be born.

SUMMARY: Dream baby, dream.

3. Judith Simmer-Brown, "The Dakini's Womb," *Tricycle: The Buddhist Review*, accessed March 30, 2026.

13

AFTERWORD: BEYOND THE MIRROR

We began our journey with Prince Prospero, a man who sought to hide from death behind a mask of decadence, only to find that his true face was the very thing he feared most. But as you close this book, you do not stand in his castle. You stand at the threshold of your own life, equipped with a new technology of the soul.

The journey through the twelve houses is not a circle, but a spiral. By identifying your **Mask** and confronting your **Ghost**, you have done what Prospero could not: you have looked into the hollow. You have recognized that the Ascendant is not a lie, but a vehicle, and that the Twelfth House is not a prison, but a wellspring of genius.

The Work does not end here. It begins.

As you move back into the world, observe the "Red Specter" of your own Twelfth House. When you feel the urge to retreat, to sabotage, or to hide, remember the patterns of your Ghost Sign. Ask yourself: *Is the Mask wearing me, or am I wearing the Mask?* You are the Architect of your own character. The gateway is open, the phantoms are named, and the mirror is clear.

GLOSSARY

The Ascendant (The Mask): The point of the birth chart marking the beginning of the First House. Rather than a superficial facade, it is the *prosopon*—the undivided manifestation of the individual's potential and the primary vehicle through which one engages with physical reality.

The Daemon: Originating from the Greek *daimon (*δαίμων), this is the tutelary spirit or "inner genius" associated with the Twelfth House. It is the carrier of destiny (the "acorn") that becomes an adversarial "Bad Daemon" only when its calling is suppressed or unlived.

Ghost Sign: The zodiacal sign residing on the cusp of the Twelfth House. It represents "encrypted wisdom"—the whispers of unclaimed genius that must be integrated in order to fulfill the potential of the Ascendant.

The Mystic Axis: The structural diameter connecting the Sixth House (Habits/The Body) and the Twelfth House (Transcendence/The Unconscious). This axis informs us that spiritual insight is inextricably linked to earthly, embodied discipline.

Same-Sign Cusp: A configuration where the Twelfth House cusp and the Ascendant share the same zodiacal sign. This acts as a psychic "amplifier," creating a monolithic archetypal theme where the individual often becomes a living symbol or "ancestor."

Saturn's Cross: A metaphor for the Saturnian principles of structure, time, and physical limitation. Like Odysseus tethered to his mast, Saturn provides the vessel that allows one to hear the Siren's Song of the infinite without undergoing ego dissolution.

The Twelfth House (The Ghost Realm): The final house of the zodiacal wheel, serving as both tomb and womb. It is the repository of karma, "passed lives" (unlived possibilities) and the site where the mask meets the divine.

Veiled Sign (Interception): A sign contained entirely within a house that does not touch a cusp. In the Twelfth House, this represents a "vault within a sanctuary"—a hidden mystery with no external "door," requiring a unique, introverted process of soul-searching to unlock.

BIBLIOGRAPHY

Arroyo, Stephen. *Astrology, Karma & Transformation: The Inner Dimensions of the Birth Chart*. San Rafael, CA: CRCS Publications, 1978.

Arroyo, Stephen. *Astrology, Psychology, and the Four Elements*. San Rafael, CA: CRCS Publications, 1975.

Bancroft, A. *Origins of the Sacred: The Way of the Sacred in Western Tradition*. London: Arkana, 1987.

Barker, Margaret. "Beyond the Veil of the Temple: The High Priestly Origin of the Apocalypses." *Scottish Journal of Theology* 51, no. 1 (1998): 1-21.

Berry, Thomas. *The Dream of the Earth*. San Francisco: Sierra Club Books, 1988.

Bringhurst, Robert. *The Elements of Typographic Style*. Version 3.2. Point Roberts: Hartley & Marks, 2004.

Britannica. "Prosopon." 2024.

Carey, George W., and Inez Eudora Perry. *The Zodiac and the Salts of Salvation*. Hollywood, Los Angeles, CA: The Carey-Perry School of the Chemistry of Life, 1932.

Charles, R. H. *The Book of Enoch*. Translated by R. H. Charles. Introduction by W. O. E. Oesterley. London: Society for Promoting Christian Knowledge, 1917.

Chartrand, Tanya L., and John A. Bargh. "The Chameleon Effect: The Perception-Behavior Link and Social Interaction." *Journal of Personality and Social Psychology* 76 (1999): 893–910.

The Chicago Manual of Style. 18th ed. The University of Chicago Press Editorial Staff. Chicago: The University of Chicago Press, 2024.

Edinger, Edward F. *The Eternal Drama: The Inner Meaning of Greek Mythology*. Boston: Shambhala, 1994.

Ehrman, Bart D. *The Lost Gospel of Judas Iscariot: A New Look at Betrayer and Betrayed*. Oxford: Oxford University Press, 2006.

Euripides. *Bacchae*. Translated by Ian Johnston. Ohio: Faenum Publishing, 2015.

Euripides. *The Bacchae and Other Plays*. Translated by Philip Vellacott. London: Penguin Classics, 1973.

Forrest, Steven. *The Inner Sky*. San Diego: ACS Publications, 1984.

Guttman, Ariel, and Kenneth Johnson. *Mythic Astrology*. St. Paul, MN: Llewellyn Publications, 1993.

Harper, Douglas. "dolphin." *Online Etymology Dictionary*. Accessed March 30, 2026.

Harper, Douglas. "narcissus." *Online Etymology Dictionary*. 2001.

Herrigel, Eugen. *Zen in the Art of Archery*. New York: Pantheon Books, 1953.

Hillman, James. *The Dream and the Underworld*. New York: Harper & Row, 1979.

Hillman, James. *The Soul's Code: In Search of Character and Calling*. New York: Random House, 1996.

Hillman, James. "The Thought of the Heart." In *Facing the Gods*, edited by James Hillman, 45–70. Irving, TX: Spring Publications, 1980.

Homer. *The Iliad*. Translated by Robert Fagles. New York: Viking, 1990.

Homer. *The Odyssey: Revised Prose Translation*. Translated by E. V. Rieu. Harmondsworth: Penguin Books, 1946.

Houlding, Deborah. *The Houses, Temples of the Sky*. London: The Wessex Astrologer Ltd, 2006.

Jacobus de Voragine. *The Golden Verses*. Translated by William Caxton. Westminster: William Caxton, 1483.

Jung, Carl G. *Man and His Symbols*. New York: Dell Publishing, 1968.

Ovid. *Metamorphoses*. 2 vols. Translated by Frank Justus Miller. Loeb Classical Library. Cambridge, MA: Harvard University Press; London: William Heinemann, 1916.

Ovid. *Metamorphoses*. Translated by A. S. Kline. Poetry in Translation, 2000.

Palmer, Leonard. *The Interpretation of Mycenaean Greek Texts*. Oxford: Clarendon Press, 1963.

Plato. "Cratylus." In *The Dialogues of Plato*. Translated by Benjamin Jowett. New York and London: Macmillan and Co., 1892.

Plato. *The Republic*. Translated by Benjamin Jowett. Oxford: Clarendon Press, 1888.

Plato. *Symposium*. Translated by Alexander Nehamas and Paul Woodruff. Indianapolis: Hackett Publishing Company, 1989.

Plato. *The Timaeus of Plato*. Edited with Introduction and Notes by R. D. Archer-Hind. London: Macmillan, 1888.

Rudhyar, Dane. *Astrological Houses: The Spectrum of Individual Experience*. Garden City, NY: Doubleday, 1972.

Simmer-Brown, Judith. "The Dakini's Womb." *Tricycle: The Buddhist Review*. Accessed March 30, 2026.

Sophocles. *Oedipus King of Thebes*. Translated by Gilbert Murray. London: George Allen & Unwin Ltd., 1911.

Welker, Glenn, ed. "Ghost Stallion." *Indigenous Peoples Literature*. 1993.

Wickenburg, Joanne. *A Journey Through the Birth Chart*. St. Paul, MN: Llewellyn Publications, 1998.

Wolkstein, Diane. *Inanna, Queen of Heaven and Earth: Her Stories and Hymns from Sumer*. New York: Harper & Row, 1983.

www.ingramcontent.com/pod-product-compliance
Lightning Source LLC
LaVergne TN
LVHW011047110826
845149LV00015B/3384

* 9 7 9 8 9 9 5 6 2 1 7 0 6 *